MARY

Human and Holy

D0456418

MARY

Human and Holy

By Antonio Bello

Foreword by
Luigi Santucci

Translated by
Paul Duggan

Pauline
BOOKS & MEDIA
Boston

Original title: *Maria: Donna dei nostri giorni.* Copyright © 1993, Edizioni San Paolo, Piazza Soncino, 5-20092 Cinisello Balsamo, Milan, Italy.

ISBN 0-8198-4810-7

Cover: Icon of Our Lady of Soufanieh, Damascus, Syria.

English edition copyright © 2000, Daughters of St. Paul

Printed and published in the U.S.A. by Pauline Books & Media, 50 Saint Pauls Avenue, Boston, MA 02130-3491.

www.pauline.org

Pauline Books & Media is the publishing house of the Daughters of St. Paul, an international congregation of women religious serving the Church with the communications media.

2 3 4 5 6 7 8   06 05 04 03 02 01

To the Most Reverend
Michael Mincuzzi
Bishop of God's holy Church

CONTENTS

Contents

FOREWORD

According to a centuries-old saying, "we can never say enough about Mary." And indeed, how much has been written and sung about the mother of Jesus—from Jacopone to Peguy, from Claudel to Eliot; from Dante to Lope de Vega, from Bernanos to Hopkins; from Petrarca to Turoldo. This is to say nothing about the saints (Bonaventure, Bernard, Bernardine) or about the obscure or anonymous persons who, with ingenuity, simplicity, or rhetoric, have praised the "Woman of paradise." Yet it is not enough; it will never be enough.

So it was for Tonino Bello, bishop of Molfetta. He spoke and wrote countless words about Mary. He gave us these thirty-one brief chapters about Mary as the companion on our journey, and we welcome them into our hearts.

In speaking of Mary (rather, to Mary), the author has used personal attributes: the sweetness, tenderness, and wonder of a vibrant poet, but also strength, passion, and courage. These attributes most moved me to respect and love Tonino Bello for his generous boldness. For years he decried and confronted the shameful aspects of our society and made a radical commitment to peace and nonviolence.

What merits of this book give it the right to crowd into the overflowing field of Marian books? I would point out the originality and the boldness of certain conjectures about the Virgin. It says, for example, that Mary went to take her Son down from the cross but earlier, beneath the cross, she had poured out her "laments as a mother...pleading for the return of the sun." Again, on the theme of the passion, the author asserts that the dying Christ rested his head on Mary's, and she, "upright under the cross, perhaps standing on a stone pedestal," thus became "his cushion at death." Bello imagines that Mary, the woman of the third day, was present before the other women not just at the appearance of the Risen One, but at the most secret event of the resurrection. Finally, the book presents Mary as displaying a boundless motherliness even toward Judas, leaving her house to dissuade him from suicide. After taking Jesus down from the cross she went to take Judas down from the tree and arranged his body in the peace of death. Although perhaps not historical, these "inventions" of an imaginative narrator can help us envision Mary in her real life.

Nonetheless, in his free and distinctive writing, the author gives us instructive fragments of catechesis. He invents for us the sanctuary of the "Madonna of Fear," where we can all take refuge "for all of us, like Mary, have experienced that most human feeling which clearly signals our limitations."

Perhaps his familiarity with Our Lady, a creature of marvelous silences, endowed Tonino Bello with a fluid and masterful eloquence in writing. On the theme of silence, read the fine piece that places in scenic settings Mary's "silences" in her encounters with God. "Woman of the New Wine" presents a reflection on the barrels, cellars, and aromas of fermenting grapes in relation to the wine theme of Cana; finally, among many other expressive gems, see the doxology addressed to Mary, "Woman of Holy Saturday."

Besides being a jewel, for me this meditation brings the most profound message and the most precious gift of these pages. It transmits to us, through the medium of the Virgin, the jubilation of Easter, calling us to an almost frenzied optimism. "What will the trees do tonight when the alleluias sound forth? Will the animals of the forest howl their concerts while the Church sings the *Exsultet?* How will the sea, breaking on the reefs, react to the news of the resurrection? Beyond the gates of the cemetery, will the tombs of the dead tremble under the full moon? Will the mountains, unseen by anyone, dance with joy around the valleys?" At that hour Mary will repeat to us, her children, "that a person is always taken down from every cross. Every human bitterness dissolves into a smile; every sin finds redemption, and even mourning garments change into vestments of joy. Help us understand that the most tragic rhapsodies lead to the first steps of the dance, and funeral hymns already contain the festive motifs of the paschal alleluia."

Mary is a contemporary, a next-door neighbor, a school and shopping companion. Perhaps this book's greatest virtue, then, is its portrayal of a woman made up of light and theological transparency, mystically watching over us, a creature who has fully lived like us in time, in the hours of each day, in the way of life God called her to.

By the end of his text, the bishop and writer, Tonino Bello, appears within his open Marian dimension. He is neither a hagiographer nor a chanter of praises. He is a singer in the most lyrical sense, yet he also brings penetrating insight into unfathomed psychological spheres of his lofty subject. He is not just "devout" but something more: he is in love, in the fullest meaning of the term. In his love for Mary, Bello humbly and joyfully associates himself with that extraordinary personage of Anatole, France: the *jongleur de Notre Dame*, who as a friar, wanted to offer the Virgin Mary no other veneration than dancing before her image—expressing his exuberant love in leaps and somersaults.

—*Luigi Santucci*

EDITOR'S NOTE

M*ary: Human and Holy*, written by Bishop Antonio Bello, contains reflective meditations on Mary in our life today. Because the author attempts to draw the reader into a prayerful conversation with Mary, he freely uses the Gospel narratives as a springboard for speculating about her life. For example, he imagines Mary seeking out Judas to forgive him after Jesus died. These extra-Scriptural, non-historic incidents are intended to help the reader consider what Mary's life may have been like. Catholic devotional writings have always permitted some latitude in this regard.

Chapter 1

AN EVERYDAY WOMAN

The fourth paragraph of the *Decree on the Apostolate of the Laity* states: "Mary lived on earth a life like anyone else's, filled with family cares and work." I cannot tell you how many times I have read that without emotion. The other evening, however, this sentence from the Second Vatican Council, quoted under an image of Mary, struck me as so bold that I looked it up to verify its authenticity—and it checked out.

So, "Mary lived on earth"—not in the clouds. Her thoughts did not dwell in the air. She acted in the concrete context of everyday life. Even though God may have often called her to the experience of ecstasy, she kept her feet on the ground. Far from being an ethereal visionary, she persistently maintained her household amid harsh daily pressures.

Yet, there is more: "She lived...a life like anyone else's," even like the life of her next-door neighbor! Mary drank water from the same well. She milled grain in the same mortar. She sat in the fresh air of the same courtyard. She too returned home tired in the evening, after gleaning in the fields. The day also came when someone said to her, "Mary, your hair is turning gray." She then looked at her reflection in the fountain and experienced the same pang of nostalgia that affects everyone who sees youth fading.

But the surprises do not end there. When we learn that Mary's life was "filled with family cares and work" just like ours, we realize that she knew the fatigue and sweat of work. This causes us to wonder if our painful everyday existence has more meaning than we might think.

Yes, she also had her problems: health, finances, relationships, changes. Who knows how many times she came away from doing the laundry with a headache or worried because fewer customers had come to Joseph's workshop? Who knows how many doors she knocked on during the olive-pressing season to look for a few days' work for Jesus? Who knows how many hours she spent trying to salvage some material from Joseph's already threadbare cloak in order to make a cape for her Son?

Like all wives, she must have had moments of crisis in her relationship with her husband; reserved as he was, he may not always have understood her silence. Like all mothers, she kept watch over her Son, hoping and fearing for him as she saw him grow into a teenager and a young man. Like all women, she too experienced the suffering of not being understood, perhaps at times not even by her two greatest loves on earth. Perhaps she also feared disappointing them, or falling short of her role. And after dissolving the torment of some immense loneliness in tears, she must have found at last the joy of supernatural communion when her family came together in prayer.

Holy Mary, an everyday woman, perhaps you alone can understand that our desire to draw you back into the limits of our earthly experience does not spring from disrespect. If we dare to take your halo away for a moment, it is only because we want to see your beauty. We turn off the spotlights that beam on you only to better measure the omnipotence of God, who has hidden the sources of light behind the shadows of your flesh.

We know well that you were destined for sailing the high seas. Yet, we want you to sail along the coast, but not to reduce you to our petty coastal trade. We want to see you close to our shores. Then we can know that we, like you, are called to adventure on the oceans of freedom.

Holy Mary, help us to understand that the most fruitful chapter of theology is not the one that places you inside the biblical or patristic writings, inside spirituality or liturgy, dogmas or art. Rather, it is the one that places you inside the house of Nazareth. There, amid kettles and looms, tears and prayers, skeins of wool and scrolls of Scripture, you experienced in the depths of your femininity a joy without regret, grief without despair, departure without return.

19

Holy Mary, free us from our longing for the extraordinary; teach us to regard daily life as a workplace where the history of salvation is built. Loosen the moorings of our fears so that, like you, we might surrender to the will of God found in the prosaic turns of time and in the slow agony of the hours. Come back to walk discreetly with us, you, who before being crowned queen of heaven, tasted the dust of our poor earth.

Chapter 2

WOMAN OF FEW WORDS

Yes, I know; it isn't a suitable invocation for a litany, but if we had to reformulate our prayers to Mary in more familiar terms, I would give her this title first: woman of few words.

Mary was a true woman—she had no spiritual "makeup." Although blessed among all women, she would pass unrecognized among them except for that raiment which God tailored for her: "clothed with the sun and crowned with stars."

Mary was a true woman and, above all, a woman of few words. It's not that she was shy or timid. It's not that she had no feelings or couldn't express them. Mary was a woman of few words because, seized by the Word, she allowed it to so permeate her being that she could easily distinguish a genuine article from a thousand imitations—an authentic voice on a bookshelf of spurious writings, a genuine painting in a stack of prints.

No human language could have held as much meaning as Mary's. It came in monosyllables as rapid as a "yes," or in whispers as brief as a "fiat," or in abandonment as complete as an "amen." It came in biblical resonance bound together by the threads of ancient wisdom, nourished by fruitful silences. Precisely because there is nothing of the orator in her, we want her to accompany us along the twists and turns of our poor life, fasting, above all, from words.

Holy Mary, woman of few words, pray for us who are incurably ill with our "super eloquence." Skilled at using words to hide rather than to reveal our thoughts, we have lost our taste for simplicity. Convinced that asserting ourselves in life means we must always talk—even when we have nothing to say—we have grown verbose and uncontrolled, skilled in spinning cobwebs so that we often fall into the dark traps of the absurd, just like flies into the spider's grasp.

Holy Mary, pray for us sinners on whose lips the word turns to dust in a whirlwind. It makes a sound, but never becomes flesh. It fills our mouths, but leaves our hearts empty. It gives us the illusion of communion, but never truly draws us to others. It leaves us with the pain of an inexpressible aridity, like the sculpted statues in fountains that no longer give water.

Holy Mary, whose supernatural grandeur hung on a simple *fiat*, pray for us sinners who are always exposed, between healing and relapse, to the intoxication of words. Protect our lips from useless exaggeration. Make our voices, reduced to essentials, always begin from the realms of mystery and bring forth the perfume of silence. Turn us, like you, into a sacrament of transparency. Help us, finally, so that in the brevity of a "yes" spoken to God, we might throw ourselves into the boundless sea of his love.

Chapter 3

WOMAN IN WAITING

True sadness settles on us not when we return home at night to find no one waiting, but when we expect nothing more. We suffer the darkest loneliness not when the fire in the hearth flickers out, but when we no longer want to rekindle it—not even for a possible guest.

True sadness comes when we think that the music will never play for us, and no one will ever knock on our door. We think we will never jump for joy over good news, and that nothing will ever surprise us again. We do not expect to shudder with grief over human tragedy, because we cannot imagine loving anyone that much. So, life runs straight into an epilogue that never arrives, like a cassette that

24

has finished and reels on without sound until it finally stops.

Waiting means experiencing a taste for living. It has been said that the depth of one's desires is the measure of holiness. Perhaps that is true. If so, then Mary is the holiest of creatures, because her whole life was paced by the joyful rhythms of a person waiting for someone else.

Luke's first words about her carry the promise of expectations: she was "engaged to a man whose name was Joseph, of the house of David" (Lk 1:27). Mary was a fianceé, then. These words allude to the harvest of hope and the stirring of the heart every person in love experiences as a prelude to mysterious tenderness. Even before the Gospel announces her name, it says that Mary was engaged. She was a virgin in waiting, waiting for Joseph, waiting for the sound of his sandals as evening approached when, perfumed by wood and varnish, he would come to talk with her about his dreams.

Yet, even in her last appearance in Scripture, the text captures Mary in an attitude of waiting. There with the disciples, in the upper room of the Cenacle, she awaited the coming of the Spirit. She listened for the rustle of his wings as the day approached when the Spirit would descend on the Church to direct its mission of salvation. Mary was a virgin in waiting at the beginning, a mother in waiting at the end. Under an arch spanning these two awesome events—one so human, the other so divine—she felt countless consuming expectations.

She waited for Jesus during nine long months. She waited for the fulfillment of the law with the offerings of the poor and the rejoicing of relatives. She waited for the day—the only day she wanted to postpone—when her Son would leave home and never come back. She waited for the "hour" when the abundance of grace would be poured out on the table of God's people. She waited for the last breath of her only-begotten Son, nailed to the cross. She waited for the third day, keeping a solitary vigil before the tomb. "To wait" is the flip side of the verb "to love." In Mary's vocabulary, to wait always meant to love.

Holy Mary, virgin in waiting, give us some of your oil, because our lamps are flickering out and we have nothing in reserve. Do not send us to other sellers. Rekindle within our hearts the old fervor that burned within when a small thing could make us leap with joy—the arrival of a friend from far away, an evening sky's red glow after a storm, the crackling of a log in wintertime, the ringing of bells on feast days, the fragrance of lavender from a burning candle.

If today we no longer know how to wait, it is because we fall short of hope. The sources have dried up. We are suffering a profound crisis of desire. Sated by the thousand substitutes surrounding us, we risk not waiting anymore for anything, not even for the eternal promises signed in blood by the God of the covenant.

Holy Mary, comfort those mothers who grieve for their children—those children who suffer illness or meet with an untimely death, children who struggle with addictions or who suffer in any way. Comfort those mothers whose children were scattered by the fury of war, overturned by the whirlwinds of passion, or shaken by the storms of life.

Holy Mary, give us a watchful heart. Standing at the beginning of the third millennium, help us to be prophets of the future. Sentinel of the morning, arouse in our hearts the passion of youth in bearing God's message to a world that already feels old. Finally, bring harp and flute for us, so that arising early with you, we might greet the dawn.

Faced with changes that are shaking history, let us feel the thrill of new beginnings. Make us understand that acceptance is not enough: we must also wait. Accepting is sometimes a sign of resignation, but waiting is always a sign of hope. Make us ministers in waiting. Virgin of advent, through your maternal assurance, may the Lord who is coming surprise us with our lamps in hand.

Chapter 4

WOMAN IN LOVE

Ti voglio bene.
Je t'aime.
Te quiero.
Ich liebe Dich.
I love you.

I don't know whether people in Mary's time used the same messages of love, tender as heartfelt prayers and short as graffiti, which teenagers use today. But even if they didn't use a ball point pen on jeans or chalk on walls, the adolescents of Palestine then probably behaved as young people now.

With the "stylus of a speedy scribe" on sycamore bark, or with the point of a shepherd's staff on sandy land, they must have had a code for communicating love to each other. This feeling, old and yet always new, shakes the soul of every human being who opens up to the mystery of life: *I love you!*

Mary too experienced this splendid season of life, filled with amazement and tears, exultation and doubts, tenderness and fearfulness, in which, as in a crystal goblet, all the perfumes of the universe seemed distilled. She savored the joy of meeting friends or waiting for feasts, the elation of dancing, the innocent joy in a compliment, delight over new clothes. It grew like a vase under the potter's hand, and everyone wondered about the mystery of that transparency without dross, that freshness without shadows.

One evening, a young man named Joseph plucked up his courage and declared, "Mary, I love you." She answered him with a thrill of excitement: "And I, you." The brilliance of all the stars in the sky shone in their eyes.

Her girlfriends, who picked flowers with her in the meadows, didn't understand how she could combine her rapture in God and her love for a creature. It was hard for those girls to put both kinds of love together. For Mary, instead, it was like putting together two halves of a line from a psalm. On the Sabbath they would see her absorbed in profound prayer and love of God as she sang in the synagogue choir: "O God, you are my God, I seek you, my soul thirsts for you...as in a dry and weary land where there is no water" (Ps 63:1). Then in the evening, as they took turns telling about the trials of love, Mary would amaze them when she spoke about her fiancé in the cadences of the Song of Songs: "My beloved is...distinguished among ten thousand.... His eyes are like doves beside springs of water.... His appearance is like Lebanon, choice as the cedars..." (Song 5:10, 12, 15).

For the other girls from Nazareth, the human love they experienced was like water in a cistern: clear, yes, but with some dregs on the bottom. It wouldn't take much to stir up the dregs and muddy the water. For Mary, no. They could never understand that Mary's love had no dregs, because hers was a bottomless well.

Holy Mary, woman in love, inextinguishable burning bush of love, we ask pardon for offenses against your humanity. We have thought you capable only of flames ascending toward heaven, and then, perhaps out of fear of contaminating you with earthly things, we have excluded you from the experience of small sparks here below. You, however, a furnace of love for the Creator, also teach us how to love creatures. Help us to see the beauty of both forms of love.

Make us understand that love is always holy, because its flames issue from the one fire of God. Help us also to understand that with the same fire, we can light lamps of joy and can burn away the most beautiful things in life.

Therefore, holy Mary, if it is true, as the liturgy sings, that you are the "Mother of fair love," accept us into your school. Teach us to love—a difficult art that we learn slowly. Help us to clear away the layers of ash from the embers without extinguishing them.

To love means to go out of one's self, to give without asking, to be discreet. It means to suffer, to shake off the scales of selfishness, to put others' needs first. It means to seek another's happiness, to respect his or her destiny, and to vanish, when the time has come to let go.

Holy Mary, help us understand what *real* love is. Help us rejoice in God's gift when love comes into our lives, and help us feel the joy of life like an underground spring that flows up and forms a great stream.

Help us understand the holiness that underlies those hidden leaps of the spirit, when our heart seems to stop or to beat more strongly before the miracle of beauty: a pastel sunset, the ocean's salty spray, rainfall in a pine grove, the last snowfall of winter, the colors of the rainbow, the harmonies of a thousand violins played by the wind.... From the subsoil of our memories a desire for peace seeps up, joining with future hopes, making us feel the presence of God.

Chapter 5

WOMAN WITH CHILD

A nd Mary remained with her about three months and then returned to her home" (Lk 1:56).

The Gospel does not say if Mary returned "with haste," as she did on going to see Elizabeth. But we can suppose so. Mary left Nazareth in a hurry, without taking leave of anyone. God's incredible call had affected her profoundly. But now it was time to go back. Three months in the mountains had given her time to carefully think over her situation. Close to Elizabeth, her child—whose secret she slowly began to unravel—completed the first stage of development.

Now she had to go home and confront the earthly problems every expectant woman faces. Yet, complications arose. How would she tell Joseph about it? How would she explain to her companions— with whom, a short while before, she had shared her dreams as a girl in love—the mystery that had emerged in her womb? What would they say in the village?

Still, she wanted to return soon to Nazareth and so she traveled quickly. Moreover, on those country trails she felt as if the wind was supporting her.

She had hardly gotten back home when Joseph, without even asking her to elaborate on what the angel had told him about the conception of Jesus, immediately took her away with himself. He was content to stay close to her, watching over her needs. He understood her concerns, her sudden moments of weariness. He helped her to prepare for the birth that drew ever closer. One night, she said to him, "Feel the baby, Joseph; he's moving." He then lightly placed his hand on her abdomen and trembled with happiness.

Mary knew the tribulations every pregnant woman goes through. It was as if all the hopes and fears of every expectant woman were concentrated in her. What will become of this fruit, not yet ripe, which I am carrying in my womb? Will people love him? Will he find happiness in life? How heavily will that verse from Genesis, "In pain you shall bring forth children" (3:16) weigh upon me?

A hundred questions without answers crept into her mind, a hundred portents of light, yet also a hundred anxieties. They swarmed over her as her female relatives kept her company late into the evening. She listened with serenity, and she would smile every time someone would whisper, "I bet it will be a girl."

Holy Mary, woman with child, in your virginal body you offered to the Eternal God a home in time. Tender vessel wherein God enclosed himself—though the heavens cannot contain him—we will never know how you spoke to him. You felt him leaping under your heart. Perhaps in those moments you asked yourself if you gave him his heartbeat, or if he lent you his.

You kept vigil with anxious dreams. While you worked at the loom with its shuttles whirring, and prepared woolen cloths for him with speedy hands, you also slowly wove him a tunic of flesh in the silence of your womb. Who knows how many times you felt a foreboding that, one day, rough soldiers would pierce that tunic? A pang of sadness would touch you then, but your smile would return upon thinking that the women of Nazareth, coming to see you after childbirth, would say, "He resembles his mother in everything."

Fountain through whom the water of life has come to us from the slopes of the eternal hills, holy Mary, help us to accept every person as a gift. No reason justifies rejecting any human person. No reason legitimates violence against the innocent. Teach us respect for the miracle of a blossoming life.

Holy Mary, we thank you because, while you carried Jesus in your womb for nine months, you carry each of us all our lives. Give us your virtues. Transform our features into those of your spirit. When our heavenly birthday arrives and the gates of heaven open wide to us, it will only be because we have come to resemble you—however slight that resemblance may be.

Chapter 6

WOMAN OF ACCEPTANCE

Vatican II's *Dogmatic Constitution on the Church* contains a phrase which stands out for its doctrine and conciseness. It says that at the angel's announcement, Mary the virgin "accepted the Word of God in her heart and her body" (n. 53).

In her heart and in her body. She was first the disciple and then the mother of the Word: disciple because she listened to the Word and kept it always in her heart, and mother because she offered her womb to the Word and kept him for nine months in the vessel of her body. As St. Augustine says, Mary was greater for having accepted the Word into her heart than for accepting it into her womb.

Perhaps words fail to help us grasp the beauty of this truth, so we need to use pictures. We can refer to a renowned icon, *Our Lady of the Sign*, that depicts Mary with her divine Son Jesus inscribed on her breast. It could also be called *Our Lady of Acceptance*, because with her forearms lifted in an attitude of offering or surrender, she appears as the living symbol of the most gratuitous hospitality.

She accepted him in her heart. She made room in her thoughts for God's thoughts, but she did not feel reduced to silence because of this. She willingly offered the virgin land of her spirit for the germination of the Word. She joyously granted him the most inviolable soil of her interior life without reducing the space of her freedom. She gave a secure dwelling to the Lord in the most secret rooms of her soul, but she did not feel his presence an intrusion.

She accepted him in her body. She felt the physical weight of another being growing in her motherly womb, so she adapted her daily rhythms to those of her guest. She modified her habits to fulfill her responsibility, one that certainly did not make her life easier. She dedicated her days to bearing a child, with all the concerns and efforts that brought. Because the blessed fruit of her womb was the Word of God made flesh for the salvation of humanity, she understood that in some mysterious way, God called on her to play a special role in that drama.

She accepted the Word of God in her heart and her body. This fundamental hospitality says much about Mary's style; the Gospel does not talk about her thousand other acts of acceptance, but we can intuit them. She never rejected anyone. Everyone found shelter under her shadow: her neighbors and old girlfriends in Nazareth, Joseph's relatives and the young friends of her Son, the poor of the region and pilgrims in transit, Peter in tears after he betrayed Jesus and the disciples who fled and hid in fear.

Holy Mary, woman of acceptance, help us to accept the Word in the intimacy of our hearts. Help us understand, as you did, how God acts in our lives. He does not knock at the door to evict us, but to fill our loneliness with light. He does not come into our house to put us in handcuffs, but to restore to us true freedom.

Yet, we fear we won't welcome the Lord who is coming. Change tires us. Since he always seems to confuse our thoughts, question our agendas, and throw our certainties into doubt, every time we hear his footsteps, we avoid him by hiding in the bushes, like Adam among the trees of Eden. Help us understand that even though God may upset our projects, he does not ruin the feast; even though he disturbs our sleep, he does not take away our peace. Once we have accepted him into our hearts, our bodies too will shine with his light.

Holy Mary, help us show hospitality to our brothers and sisters. In these difficult times, the danger of being cheated by malice makes us live behind barred doors and security systems. We no longer trust one another but see traps everywhere. Suspicion overshadows our relations with our neighbors. The fear of being betrayed has won out over the drive for solidarity that we still bear within us. Our hearts are divided into pieces behind the gates in our neighborhoods.

We pray you to dispel our mistrust. Help us get out of the trench of our group selfishness and break down barriers. Open our hearts to people different from ourselves. Remove our borders—the cultural before the geographical ones. The latter must yield to the rush of "other" peoples, but the former sometimes refuses to yield. Since we are forced to accept strangers into our cities, help us also to accept them into the heart of our society.

Holy Mary, monstrance of Jesus' body taken down from the cross, receive us when we have surrendered our spirit. Give to our death the trusting quiet of one resting his head on his mother's shoulder and falling peacefully asleep. Hold us for awhile on your lap, just as you have held us in your heart all our lives. Perform over us the rituals of final purification. Carry us at last in your arms to the Eternal One. If you present us, we will surely find mercy.

Chapter 7

WOMAN WHO TAKES THE FIRST STEP

I would have to ask Scripture scholars about this since I cannot explain why in the Greek text, that word, *anastàsa,* which to me seems laden with allusions, does not come through in our translation.

Luke says that after the angel left Nazareth, "Mary set out and went with haste to a Judean town in the hill country" (Lk 1:39). After the word, "Mary," the Greek text has a participle: *anastàsa,* which means literally, "got up." Could it be a stereotypical expression, just another repetitive term, which serves as a link to other words? If so, its omission in our translations would be fully justified.

Yet the word *anastàsa* has the same root as the noun *anastàsis,* the classic term referring to the central event of our faith, the Lord's resurrection. Thus, it could easily be translated as "risen." Considering Luke's rereading of the infancy of Jesus in light of the paschal events, is it really inaccurate to imagine that the word *anastàsa* is something more than an inexpressive stereotype? Is it too daring to think that it alludes to Mary as a symbol of the "risen" Church who, in all haste, sets out to bring joyful news to the world? Is it too much to affirm that this word sums up the Church's missionary task, namely, that the Church has the task of carrying Jesus Christ in her womb to offer him to others, just as Mary did to Elizabeth?

I am dropping the matter there. However, even if the word *anastàsa* does not have the theological significance I have suggested, it does underline one thing: Mary's resoluteness. She decides to move first; no one asks her. She herself undertakes the journey; no one suggests it to her. She resolves to take the first step; she doesn't wait for other people to take the initiative.

From the angel's discreet allusion, she intuited that her cousin was having difficulties. So, without wasting any time or asking whether it was her business to go ahead, she packed her bag and went! She made the arduous journey through the mountains of Judea. She went "with haste," or, as one translation has it, "with concern."

All these elements help us understand Mary's enterprising style, which we see again at the wedding in Cana. After sensing the newlyweds' distress, and although they didn't ask, she made the first move to "checkmate" the king. Dante Alighieri was indeed right in saying that the Virgin helps not only those who turn to her, but "many times she freely anticipates our plea."

Holy Mary, woman who takes the first step, gentle minister of God's anticipatory grace, "rise up" again in haste and help us. We need you. Do not wait for our plea, but anticipate our cry for mercy. Guide us in all our initiatives.

When sin pierces and paralyzes our life, do not wait for our repentance but anticipate our cry for help. Run swiftly to our side and stir up hope in our hearts despite our misdeeds. If you do not help us on time, we will lie in the mud. If you do not open up wells of repentance in our hearts, we will never feel our need for God.

Holy Mary, how many times you must have amazed people during your earthly life by always being the first to forgive. With how much concern, after suffering an offense from some neighbor, you "rose up" first to knock on her door, listen to her distress, and embrace her. With how much tenderness, on the night of your Son's betrayal, you "rose up" to cover Peter's bitter lament with your cloak. And with what anxiety you must have learned of Judas' betrayal and "rose up" to search him out to offer the hope of forgiveness. I imagine that, after taking Jesus down from the cross, you also went to take Judas down from the tree and arranged his body in the peace of death.

We pray you, give us the strength to make the first move when we need to forgive. Make us, like yourself, experts at taking the first step. Don't let us put off till tomorrow an encounter of peace that we can carry out today. Shake us out of our indecision.

Free us from the narrowness of expecting others to act first. Help us to never force another to stand on hot coals while we scornfully repeat, "It's his turn to make the first move!"

Holy Mary, woman skilled in making the first move, anticipate our judgment in God's heart as well. For when we knock on heaven's gate and appear before the Eternal One, let your sentence come first. "Rise up" again from your throne of glory and come to meet us. Take our hand and cover us with your mantle. With a lamp of mercy in your eyes, anticipate his verdict of grace, and forgiveness will be ours. For God's greatest happiness is to ratify what you have decided.

Chapter 8

MISSIONARY WOMAN

Scripture scholars say that the oldest Marian text in the New Testament is found in Galatians: "When the fullness of time had come, God sent his Son, born of a woman..." (Gal 4:4). Even in its restraint, this passage expresses a momentous idea. Not only does it tell us about seasons already ripe for the redemption, but with the phrase "born of a woman," it makes us understand two crucial things: the grafting of the Eternal onto the stock of humanity, and the grafting of Mary in God's salvific plan.

However, this text impresses me not so much because of its explicit affirmation of Mary's divine maternity, but because it shows that from her first step onto the vast biblical stage, Mary appears alongside a missionary. The text presents Jesus Christ as the great One sent by God. The verb "I send" is the typical term indicating mission; it qualifies in the clearest way the Son as the Father's apostle.

Is it not marvelous, then, that Mary appears to us in the history of salvation as closely associated with the great missionary, as if to signify that the basic feature of her maternal image is that of mission? Indeed, several Gospel passages show Mary's missionary function more concretely.

It suffices to reflect on her visit to Elizabeth. The Virgin went with haste, as if she felt the urgency of the same word that summoned the angel Gabriel to carry the good news to Nazareth. "The Angel Gabriel was sent by God...." He was *sent!* This verb has a strong impact. Not only was the angel sent to earth, but Mary, caught up in this dynamism, also set out on her journey toward the heights of Judea. She was also *sent*. At the beginning of her trip, we find again the typical missionary verb. Mary obeyed that impulse. Carrying Christ in her womb, she became the first monstrance for him; as if inaugurating

Corpus Christi processions, she carried the news of liberation to her faraway relatives.

In this and other texts, we can consider Mary as the messenger of the good news. It seems to me, however, that to perceive her missionary dimension, no biblical episode can match the rich theological power of her emergence alongside Christ as Galatians describes.

Holy Mary, missionary woman, grant to your Church the joy of rediscovering the roots of her primordial vocation. Help her to measure herself by Christ and by no other, as you did when, appearing at the dawn of New Testament revelation alongside him, you chose him as the only measure of your life.

When the Church lingers within her tents where the cry of the poor does not resound, give her the courage to go outside the encampment. When she is tempted to settle into a comfortable life, take her out of that apparent security. When she gets accustomed to familiar ways of doing things, shake her

out of that sedentary life. Sent by God for the salvation of the world the Church must walk, not settle
down.

50

A nomad like yourself, place in her heart a great
passion for human beings. A pregnant virgin like
you, guide her in the paths of suffering. A wander-
ing mother like you, fill her with tenderness toward
all the needy. Help her to burn with zeal for showing Jesus Christ, as you did to the shepherds, to
Simeon, to the magi from the East, and to countless
other nameless individuals awaiting redemption.

Holy Mary, we pray to you for all those who have
left behind their dearest affections in order to proclaim the Gospel in distant lands. They have felt
more than others the piercing fascination of that icon
which portrays you along with Christ, the Father's
special messenger. Sustain them in their toil. Give
them rest from their weariness. Protect them from
every danger. As they bend over the wounds of the
poor, help them to act with your tenderness. Put
words of peace on their lips. Do not let their hopes,
by which earthly justice is fostered, betray the supernatural expectations of a new heaven and a new

earth. Fill their loneliness and soften the pangs of nostalgia in their hearts. When they need to cry, offer them your motherly shoulder on which to rest their heads. Make them witnesses of joy. Every time they return home, help us all to measure up to their enthusiasm. May their example spur us on to more sensitive pastoral action and greater generosity.

Holy Mary, invigorate our Christian life with the ardor that drove you, bearer of the light, into the roads of Palestine. Flask of the Spirit, pour out his chrism on us, so that you might place in our hearts the desire to go to the "far reaches of the earth."

Even if life ties us to the place where we were born, let us feel on our necks the breath of the multitudes that do not yet know Jesus. Open our eyes to see the world's suffering. Do not shield us from the clamor of the poor, even if it disturbs our peace.

You, who in the home of Elizabeth uttered the most beautiful song of liberation, inspire in us the boldness of the prophets. Let words of hope ring true on our lips. Help us gladly pay the price of our faithfulness to the Lord, and deliver us from resignation.

Chapter 9

WOMAN WHO TOOK SIDES

Mary took sides. We only have to read the *Magnificat* to realize that she did not remain neutral. She sided with the poor, the marginalized, and the downtrodden of all ages. She sided with those discriminated against by human malice, those pushed aside by the power of destiny, and all those who count for nothing in the eyes of history.

I do not advocate certain interpretations that favor a purely political reading of the *Magnificat*. This would greatly reduce the horizons of Mary's sentiments, for she sang of a liberation more profound and lasting than those brought about by mere social revolts. Its prophetic accents go beyond earthly justice while still including it, and lash out at far more radical evils.

On the historical level, however, Mary made a very specific choice. She took the side of the downtrodden. She decided to play for the losing team. She chose to wave the flag of the oppressed rather than brandish the pennants of rulers. She enrolled, as it were, in the army of the poor, yet did not turn weapons on the rich. Rather, she invited them to desert their encampments and join her in her song of compassion.

Thus did she exalt God's mercy. She revealed to us that God defends the humble and scatters the proud in the thoughts of their hearts. He stretches out his arm on behalf of the weak and topples the violent from their places of power. He fills the hungry with good things and sends the wealthy away empty-handed.

Some may find this discriminatory. They may wonder how Mary can side with the poor if her love is universal. What of her acknowledged tenderness toward sinners, among whom are the proud, the powerful, and the ruthless?

The answer is complex. Yet it becomes clear when we reflect that Mary is not like certain mothers who want to live quietly and so give in to their children's every whim. They think they will avoid problems if they abet the outrages of their wildest children. No. Mary takes a position, without ambiguity and without half measures. However, she neither takes a position in the fortress of class struggle nor in the trenches of group interests. She does so only on the terrain where she expects that someday, with their conflicts resolved, all her children might become brothers and sisters and at last find true liberation.

Holy Mary, woman who took sides, how far we are from your logic! You trusted in God and like him risked everything for the poor, standing alongside them and making poverty the clearest sign of your total abandonment to God. He "...chose what is foolish in the world to shame the wise; God chose what is weak in the world to shame the strong; God chose what is low and despised in the world, things that are not, to reduce to nothing things that are" (1 Cor 1:27–28). But we depend more on security. We fear taking risks. We want to insure ourselves against the unexpected. The Lord's risky methods are more just, but we prefer the earthly practicality of our programs. Thus, while proclaiming the paradoxes of God, we continue to rely on power and prestige, money and shrewdness, success and strength.

When will we decide to follow your example and make choices that involve loss on a natural level with the conviction that only by crossing over to your shore can we find salvation?

Holy Mary, free us from the temptation to serve two masters. Make us go out into the open. Don't let us try to reconcile impossible opposites. Preserve us from the sacrilege of legitimizing—through a misunderstanding of the sense of Christian universality—violence that harms the oppressed. Help us to feel a just shame when we compromise the truth for fear of offending the powerful or losing their favor. Help us feel a holy anger toward injustice and those who commit it.

Holy Mary, we pray to you for the Church of God. Help all Christians to align themselves courageously with the poor. The Church proclaims the "preferential option" on their behalf; may we never compromise that commitment. The Church must be the critical conscience condemning the structures of sin, which crush the defenseless and push so many people down to subhuman levels. Inspire accents of confidence in her, and place on her lips the challenging words of the *Magnificat*. Only in this way will she be able to give a living witness to truth and liberty, to justice and peace. Then human beings will open themselves once more to the hope of a new world, just as it happened on that day two thousand years ago on the mountains of Judah.

Chapter 10
WOMAN OF THE FIRST LOOK

Yes, she was the first one to lay eyes on the human face of God. She wrapped him immediately with her gaze, even before wrapping him in swaddling clothes to contain the light of that body so it would not blind her.

See him there, the one awaited by the nations whom Mary was the first to behold. The patriarchs had looked for his arrival since ancient times, but they did not have the joy of seeing him. In words laden with mystery, the prophets described his face, but their eyes closed before they could gaze upon him.

The poor had experienced a thousand shocks at every hopeful burst of messianic news, but each time they had to content themselves with pursuing him in their dreams. On winter nights as fire crackled in their shelters, shepherds spoke of the one who was to come. While they fed the fire with branches, their eyes glistened with anticipation.

On spring evenings, thick with prophecies, parents showed children the stars of heaven and sang them a lullaby with the cadences of ancient elegies: "O, if you would only open the heavens and come down to us!" Then they too would close their eyes, tired of gazing.

The eyes of old people and babies, the eyes of exiles and the oppressed, the eyes of sufferers and dreamers—how many eyes sought for him! They wanted only to see his face. Although delays disappointed them and they grew tired of long vigils, they still felt inflamed with hope that God would hear their anguished plea: "Show us your face!"

See him there at last, Emmanuel, bathed in the tears of childbirth, which glistened like gems in the flickering light. Mary's eyes looked with love over her newborn child and in their depths the long chain of unfulfilled glances of the past burned once again.

Her eyes reflect the hopes of centuries-old expectations, stir flames lurking under the ashes of time.

Mary becomes the woman of the first look. Only a creature like Mary could worthily welcome the Son of God on earth, greeting him with eyes that radiated holiness. After her, many others would have the privilege of seeing him. Joseph would see him, then the shepherds. Later, Simeon would see him and then die in peace because his eyes had contemplated the salvation of God....

Mary, wrapping him with the warmth of her gaze on a night perfumed with moss and the stable, was the woman chosen beforehand, from everlasting ages, to be—after countless expectations—the gleaming bank washed by the stream of grace.

Holy Mary, woman of the first look, grant us the grace of wonder. The world has robbed us of that capacity. Excitement has faded from our eyes. We've grown weary of keeping vigil, because we expect no more arrivals. Our souls have withered like a dried-up riverbed where the deep levels of wonder have been drained out. Victims of boredom, we lead arid lives deprived of ecstasy. Things we've already seen move before our eyes like movie reruns. We live through seasons without the first fruits of the harvest. Instead, we think we already know what flavor each fruit conceals under its rind. You experienced God's surprises, now restore to us, we pray you, the desire that God might touch our lives too, and give us the joy of experiencing his love anew.

Holy Mary, give us the grace of tenderness. You always carried in your pure eyes the shimmering of God's transparency, now help us so that we too might experience the entire truth of Jesus' words: "The eye is the lamp of the body. So, if your eye is healthy, your whole body will be full of light" (Mt 6:22).

Holy Mary, we thank you because, as you bend over your child, you represent us all. You are the first creature to have contemplated the flesh of God made man, and we want to look out of the window of your eyes to enjoy the first fruits with you. You are also the first creature on earth that God saw with his eyes of flesh, and we want to cling to your garments to share this privilege with you.

Thank you, incomparable friend of our Christmas celebrations, hope of our loneliness, comfort of our chilly mangers without choirs of angels or crowds of shepherds. Forgive us if our looks have turned elsewhere, if we pursue other faces, if we run after other appearances. Know that, in the depth of our souls, the longing for that look still remains, or rather, for *those* looks—yours and his. Now cast a glance on us also, Mother of Mercy, especially when we find that no one is left to love us except you.

Chapter 11

WOMAN OF THE BREAD

She "laid him in a manger" (Lk 2:7). Within the space of a few lines, Luke repeats the word "manger" three times. Luke is hinting, no doubt. He, the painter, wants to portray Mary as someone filling the empty basket on the table. Although fodder for animals is put into a manger, we can read into this image the intention of presenting Jesus, from his first appearance, as the food of the world—as the bread of the world.

Underneath him lay the hay for beasts on top of the hay lay the grain that was milled and baked for humanity. In the manger, wrapped in cloths like clean towels, lay the Living Bread come down from heaven.

Alongside the manger, Mary knelt as if before a tabernacle. She had understood well her role since the time she saw Providence lead her far from her town to give birth in Bethlehem, which means "house of bread."

Accordingly, on the night they were turned away she used the manger as a breadbasket for the table. In a sense Mary anticipated, through this prophetic gesture, Jesus' call on the night he was betrayed, a call addressed to the whole world: "Take this, all of you, and eat it: this is my body which will be given up for you" (Lk 22:19).

Mary is the bearer of bread and not merely of a spiritual sort. She too felt the human concern of putting food on the table; yes, she worked hard for material bread. Perhaps sometimes, when she could not get it, she cried in secret. Jesus must have read in his mother's shining eyes her torment over the missing bread, as well as her delight over its aroma when she took it hot from the oven and broke it over the table into many pieces.

For this reason, the Gospel celebrates bread: when divided it is multiplied, and when passed from hand to hand it satisfied the hunger of the poor reclining on the grass and still overflowed twelve baskets with leftovers.

So in his prayer addressed to the Father, Jesus gave us the plea for daily bread. And we also implore the mother of grace for its fair distribution, so that none of her children go hungry.

Holy Mary, woman of the bread, how many times in Nazareth did you feel the poverty of your table? Did you wish it were more worthy of the Son of God? Like all mothers concerned to provide for their children, you worked hard so that Jesus would have a plate of beans at your table or a handful of figs in his tunic pockets.

Your bread came through sweat, not through having much money. Joseph worked hard, putting in long hours at his carpenter's workshop. He was happy when he could finish a bench and perhaps barter it for a sack of grain. On baking days, when the warm fragrance of bread drifted into his shop, Joseph would hear you singing, and Jesus, watching you at the breadboard, perhaps thought of his future parable: "The kingdom of heaven is like yeast that a woman took and mixed in with three measures of flour..." (Mt 13:33).

Holy Mary, you suffered like everyone who must struggle to survive. Reveal to us a sense of the misery of the poor. Have mercy on the millions of people who suffer from hunger, and make us sensitive to the challenge of their cry. Do not spare us from the distress of seeing the children whom death snatches while they tragically cling to their mothers' dry breasts. Let every piece of our leftover bread call into question our trust in the current economic order, which seems to only guarantee the resources of the strongest.

Mary, ease the tears of the poor who must leave their native countries. Temper their loneliness; shield them from the humiliation of rejection. Tinge with hope the expectations of the unemployed. Curb the selfishness of those who are already comfortably set up at the banquet of life. The table does not lack food, but we lack the desire to share it.

Holy Mary, did you teach Jesus the phrase from

Deuteronomy by which he put the tempter to shame in the desert: "One does not live by bread alone, but by every word that comes from the mouth of God" (Mt 4:4)? Repeat this phrase for us, because we easily forget it. Make us understand that bread cannot fill our souls and that bank accounts cannot make us happy. A food-laden table does not satisfy us if truth does not fill our hearts. Without peace of soul, even a banquet cannot satisfy our hunger.

When you see us groping unsatisfied around our pantries stacked with goods, have compassion on us, soothe our need for happiness, and return to place the Living Bread come down from heaven into the manger, as you did that night in Bethlehem. For only the one who eats of that bread will never hunger in eternity.

Chapter 12

EMIGRANT WOMAN

Scarcely has Mary appeared on the stage of salvation than we see her ready to cross over boundaries. Like any emigrant, she had to undergo the tribulations that affect those forced to leave their homeland. She had to cross the border not to seek employment but to find political asylum. The angel gave Joseph a clear order: "Get up, take the child and his mother, and flee to Egypt, and remain there until I tell you; for Herod is about to search for the child, to destroy him" (Mt 2:13).

So, she arrived at the border of Egypt. On one side, she saw the last red earth of Canaan, and on the other, the first sands of the Pharaohs. See her there, trembling like a hunted doe. True, she enjoyed the right to live anywhere from the moment she cradled in her arms the child whose dominion extends "...from sea to sea and from the River to the ends of the earth!" (Ps 72:8). Yet, she also realized the risks of traveling to a foreign country.

The Gospel does not leave us even a line about that dramatic moment. We can imagine Mary, fearful yet courageous, standing at the watershed of two diverse cultures. That image is a powerful icon today for anyone who must adjust to new customs and new languages.

In her departure from the biblical scene, Mary again stands out as an emigrant woman. She was present at the Cenacle when the Holy Spirit, descending on the members of the newborn Church, made them "...witnesses...to the ends of the earth" (Acts 1:8).

We do not know if she, in following John, had to cross borders once again. According to one tradition, she ended her days in the city of Ephesus, another foreign land. One thing is certain: on Pentecost, Mary became mother to "a great multitude... from every nation, from all tribes and peoples and languages" (Rev 7:9).

In a still more powerful moment, Mary stands out, in all her symbolic grandeur, as an emigrant woman: the moment of the cross. That wood not only smashed the walls of separation dividing Jews from Gentiles, making the two into one people (cf. Eph 2:14), but also reconciled the human race with God in the one flesh of Christ. The cross represents the final line of demarcation between heaven and earth, the open border between time and eternity. Over this supreme border, human history enters into the divine story of salvation. Mary stood at that border and bathed it with her tears.

Holy Mary, emigrant woman, in the history of salvation you always appear standing at borderlines, poised not to separate but to join different worlds that confront each other. You stand at the watershed between the two covenants. You are the morning star, the dawn preceding the Sun of justice, the horizon joining the last traces of night and the first glimmer of day. In you, as St. Paul states, the "fullness of time" arrives in which God decides to be born "of a woman" (Gal 4:4). In your person, then, a chronological process centered on God's initial revelation concludes, and from it ripens another centered on the revelation of the Son.

Holy Mary, thank you for standing near the cross of Jesus. Lifted outside of the realm of the ordinary, this cross synthesizes the horizons of history and symbolizes what the world most fears—death. Yes, it is also the border place where the future breaks itself into the present, flooding it with hope.

We need this hope. Put yourself, then, at our side as we live through this age of transition. We are discovering the boundaries of our secular civilizations. Crowding at the crossroads, we see ourselves as the protagonists of a dramatic epochal passage. Massed at the dividing line where cultures branch off, we hesitate to discard the boundary markers that up to now have protected our identities. The "new things" frighten us, things that the multitudes of the poor, the oppressed, and the refugees force us to come to grips with. To defend ourselves against unwanted immigrants, we tighten our security measures. We find it more tempting to close our borders than to open our hearts. So, we need you, that hope might always take first place and that fear of the future might not overcome us.

Holy Mary, from ancient times Christians have invoked you with the title, "Gate of Heaven," knowing that you guard the passage between heaven and earth. At the hour of our death, remain near us in our loneliness as you did for Jesus. Watch over us in our agonies, and do not leave our side. At the final line that separates our exile from our homeland, stretch out your hand to us. For if you meet us at the decisive threshold of our salvation, we will pass safely over the border.

Chapter 13

COURAGEOUS WOMAN

From the moment when the Angel Gabriel told her, "Do not be afraid," Mary faced life with an incredible strength of spirit. She became the "mother of our age," symbol for all time. She also had to deal with fear: fear of not being understood, fear of human malice, fear for Joseph's health, fear for Jesus' lot, fear of remaining alone.... How many fears!

If we built a shrine to "Our Lady of Fear," we could all take refuge in it. All of us, like Mary, have experienced that most human feeling which clearly signals our limitations.

We all face fears: fear of tomorrow, fear that a love cultivated over many years might end unexpectedly, fear for the son who drifts through life and is already over thirty, fear for the youngest girl in the house who stays out late drinking and who refuses to talk about how she feels. We face fears about our declining health, old age, the night, death....

So in the shrine to "Our Lady of Fear," praying before Mary who has become "Our Lady of Trust," each one of us would regain the strength to go forward. We could recall the verses of a psalm which Mary must have prayed many times: "Even though I walk through the darkest valley, I fear no evil; for you are with me...my whole life long..." (Ps 23:4, 6).

Mary is "Our Lady of Fear," then, but not of resignation. She never let her arms fall as a sign of quitting, or raised them in a gesture of surrender. She surrendered only once: when she uttered her *fiat* and offered herself as a servant of her Lord.

From then on, she always responded with incredible determination, moving against the current and overcoming unheard-of difficulties that would have crippled anyone else. No sooner had she faced the hardship of giving birth in a stable than she had to flee into exile, escaping Herod's persecution. She heard the prophecy of Simeon, laden with dreadful foreboding. She endured the sacrifices of a poor life spent in thirty years of silence, then watched Jesus leave her when he closed the carpenter's workshop, fragrant with varnish and memories. Anguished by news about her son, she followed him to Calvary where, defying the violence of the soldiers and the scorn of the crowd, she bravely took her place beside the cross.

Mary faced a difficult test, marked—as it was for her dying son—by the silence of God. Her test had no lovely scenes and never skimped on suffering. This explains the antiphon sometimes chanted on Good Friday: "O all you who pass by this way, stop and see if there is any suffering like my suffering" (Lam 1:12).

Holy Mary, courageous woman, in a noted homily given in 1979 at the Basilica of Our Lady of Zapopán, México, John Paul II sculpted the most beautiful monument that the magisterium of the Church has ever raised to your human tenacity. He said that you showed yourself to be a model "for those who do not

accept passively the adverse circumstances of personal and social life, and are not victims of 'alienation.'"

You did not resign yourself to suffer injustice. You
struggled. You confronted obstacles with open eyes.
You reacted directly to your personal difficulties and
rebelled against the social injustices of your time.
You were not a saccharine woman as some devotional images portray you. You went into the street
and faced dangers there, knowing that your privileges as the Mother of God would not shelter you
from the violence of life.

Holy Mary, in the three hours of agony beside the
cross, you absorbed the afflictions of all mothers on
earth; give us something of your strength. Comfort
those women who, in the intimacy of their homes,
suffer any kind of abuse. In the name of God, the
defender of the poor, support all whose dignity is
threatened or abused. Help them to rise up against
cruelty and injustice. Lighten the pains of all victims of violence and oppression.

Holy Mary, you gained the palm of martyrdom
on Calvary even without dying, encourage us by
your example to stand fast even in adversity. Help

us to carry the burden of our daily trials not with despair, but with the serenity of those who know that God holds them in the palm of his hand. If we feel tempted to despair because we can no longer stand it, come to our side. Sit down next to us on our bleak sidewalk, speaking over and over your words of hope.

Then, comforted by your presence, we will invoke you with the oldest known prayer in your honor: "Beneath your protection we seek refuge, holy Mother of God; do not despise our pleas in our necessities, but free us from every danger, O glorious and blessed Virgin." Amen.

Chapter 14

WOMAN ON THE MOVE

If the characters in the Gospel had carried some kind of pedometer, I believe Mary would have won in the category of the most tireless walker—except for Jesus, of course. He was so identified with the road that on one occasion he confided to the disciples: "I am the way" (Jn 14:6). He is the way, not a wayfarer!

Since Jesus is outside the competition, Mary undoubtedly heads the list of evangelical travelers. We always find her on the move, from one place to another in Palestine and even abroad.

She journeyed from Nazareth to the mountains of Judah and back to visit her cousin Elizabeth. Luke lets us know Mary moved rapidly: "Mary set out and went with haste to a Judean town" (Lk 1:39). Other journeys followed: first to Bethlehem, the clandestine exile in Egypt, then to Jerusalem for the presentation in the temple, the wary return to Judea on the advice of the Lord's angel, and then back to Nazareth. She made a pilgrimage to Jerusalem, but had to retrace the route to search for Jesus. Years later, she followed Jesus amid the crowd, hearing him preach as he toured the villages of Galilee. Her pilgrimage finally led her to Calvary, to the foot of the cross. The wonder John expressed in the phrase "she was standing," portrays her greatest act of surrender to the Father's plan.

The icon of "moving forward," we find her seated only at the banquet of the first miracle—sitting, but not still. She could not stay quiet. Perhaps she did not run with her body, but she ran ahead with her soul. Mary was always on the move, going ever upward. She always aimed for the heights, from the time she set out for "the hill country," to the day of Golgotha, and to the time she went with the apostles "to the room upstairs," awaiting the Spirit.

She also descended; John records that, after the wedding at Cana, Jesus *"went down* to Capernaum with his mother" (Jn 2:12). But, the Gospel's emphasis on the verb "to go up" in connection with Jesus' journeys to Jerusalem also suggests that Mary's earthly pilgrimage is symbolic of all the toil of a demanding spiritual journey.

Holy Mary, woman on the move, how we wish to be like you in our exhausting race toward eternal life. Like you, we journey as pilgrims through life. We run faster than you, but the desert swallows our steps. If we walk on snow, our tracks soon melt away.

Forced to walk onward, we can't find a road map to make sense out of our wanderings. Even with all the highways available, our life still seems to go nowhere, our wheels spin futilely and we find ourselves stuck in the same spot.

Give us a zest for life. Make us savor the excitement of things. Give us maternal answers to our questions about the meaning of our journey. And, if under our heavy tires the flowers no longer bloom as they did under your bare feet, at least help us to slow down our frantic racing so as to enjoy their perfume and admire their beauty.

Holy Mary, make our paths lead us to communion with others, and never let us insulate ourselves within our solitude. Free us from the hectic pace of modern living and give us God's patience, which makes us slow down and wait for our traveling companions. Our hectic pace prods us to pass people by. We might gain time, but we lose the friend traveling alongside us. Our haste fills our veins with the frenzy of speed, but empties our days of tenderness. It makes us accelerate, but unlike your actions, does not give to ours the savor of charity. It deprives us of the joy of those brief contacts which, to be truly human, spill over into a hundred words.

Holy Mary, "sign of certain hope and consolation for God's pilgrim people" (*Lumen Gentium*, n. 68), make us understand that we should search for the caravan routes of our pilgrimages on the tables of history, not on geographical maps. Our faith will increase on such a spiritual journey.

Take our hand and help us discern the sacramental presence of God within the thread of our days.
Help us to recognize it in the happenings of time, in
the passing of human seasons, in the sunsets of
earthly power, in the morning glow of new peoples,
in the hope of solidarity that hangs in the air.

Guide our steps toward these sanctuaries, so that
we might find on shifting sands the traces of the
eternal. Restore to us the savor of interior searching
in place of our restlessness as aimless tourists.

If you see us skidding onto the side of the road,
stop like the Samaritan and pour over our wounds
the oil of consolation and the wine of hope. Then
put us back on our journey. Through the fog of this
"valley of tears," in all our afflictions, turn our eyes
toward the mountains from where our help comes.
On our roads the exultation of the *Magnificat* will
then flourish, just as it did in that far-off spring, on
the hills of Judea when you ascended them.

Chapter 15

WOMAN OF REST

This title was not suggested by Raphael's painting, *Our Lady of the Chair*, although that canvas certainly evokes a constellation of images centered around the mother rocking the baby resting in her arms. Surely, Mary, like all mothers, calmed her crying baby by cradling him tenderly and hugging him to her breast. She must have sung old Eastern melodies to help him sleep and then watched carefully over his peaceful slumber.

However, the title "Our Lady of Rest," is derived more from the image of Joseph sleeping peacefully near Mary than from Jesus sleeping in her arms. Only near a woman like Mary could a man like Joseph, accustomed to the harshness of life, rest with such serenity as to dream uninterruptedly.

As we know, the carpenter of Nazareth was a man of dreams. By day, he faced the hard, rough, and endless work of the workshop filled with customers and problems. At night, he deservedly withdrew into a bit of heaven, serene and inexpressible, filled with angels and portents.

Undoubtedly Mary gained this recompense for him. She not only lightened his daytime weariness by kind attention at the table, but fostered a serene atmosphere of rest which led him effortlessly into that supernatural world where she constantly dwelled. Who knows how many times she said to Joseph: "How are you feeling? You look tired. Don't wear yourself out so much. Rest awhile."

Perhaps Jesus learned this sort of kindness from her and used it later with his apostles. Seeing how tired they were, he said to them: "Come away to a deserted place all by yourselves and rest awhile" (Mk 6:31). He invited the crowds, worn out by life's toil, with these words: "Come to me, all you that are weary and are carrying heavy burdens, and I will give you rest" (Mt 11:28).

Popular tradition has so deeply understood Mary's maternal attitude that it has built up a boundless repertoire of Christmas melodies in that the most basic of musical genres: the lullaby. "Sleep in heavenly peace…." I think composers do not lend their voices to Mary so as to pacify Jesus, but so as to feel themselves cradled in her motherly arms.

Holy Mary, woman of rest, shorten those nights when we cannot sleep. How we are drained by such nights! These nights are like runways without lights where land the dark convoys of our memories and out of which stream swarms of nightmares to beset our hearts.

On these nights, the dogs barking in the street seem to give voice to the groaning of the universe, and the tolling of a clock tower drops down like hammer blows. The pendulum in the hallway marks the seconds and clocks the unstoppable march of time, dragging out the torment of hours that never end.

Watch over the rest of those who live alone. Lengthen the curtains of sleep, so often short and light as tissue over fruit, for the elderly. Lighten the burdens of those who cannot sleep because of pain. With the peace that comes from God, calm the restlessness of those who toss and turn all night because of remorse. Tuck in the rags of those sleeping under bridges, and warm the cardboard where the homeless take shelter from the cold sidewalk.

Holy Mary, we pray to you for those who proclaim the Gospel. At times, they are tired and discouraged, and they seem to say, like St. Peter, "...we have worked all night long but have caught nothing!" (Lk 5:5). When their pastoral generosity leads them to neglect themselves, remind them of their duty of rest. Draw them away from frenzied action, for apostolic stress is not a pleasing incense in God's presence.

When they pray Psalm 127 in the breviary, sing along with them, and raise your voice at the verse that says, "It is in vain that you rise up early and go late to rest, eating the bread of anxious toil; for he gives sleep to his beloved" (v. 2). They will then understand that you are not calling them to drop their commitments but to place everything in the hands of him who makes human work fruitful.

Holy Mary, help us to appreciate our Sunday rest. If others hurry out before the last blessing, help us to rediscover the ancient joy of tarrying in the churchyard, conversing with our friends, not looking at the clock. Put a brake on our exhausting timetables. Keep us far from the agitation of those who constantly struggle with time. Above all, make us understand that if the secret of physical rest lies in the weekly pauses or annual vacations we grant ourselves, then the secret of interior peace lies in knowing how to lose time with God. He loses a lot of it with us, as do you.

Even if we are late, always wait for us at the front door in the evening, after we have run around foolishly. If we find no other cushion, you offer us your shoulder, and at last we will sleep in peace.

Chapter 16

WOMAN OF THE NEW WINE

Recent biblical research has cast new light on the episode of the wedding at Cana, especially regarding Mary's role. This Gospel passage highlights the sensitivity of Jesus' mother: with thoroughly feminine finesse, she sensed the newlyweds' anxiety over running out of wine. She then forced her son's hand, saving the couple from obvious embarrassment.

It seems certain, however, that the evangelist's intention was not so much to show Mary's concern for people, or the power of her intercession with her son. Rather, it was to present her as the woman who instantly perceived that the old world had reached its term. Anticipating the "hour" of Jesus, she introduced into the banquet of history not only the jars of the feast, but also the first fermentation of newness.

Feast and newness, then, burst upon the scene at her express appeal. To confirm this for us, John's text notes a significant detail: there were *six* stone jars, used for Jewish purification rites. Because there were *six* of them—not seven, the perfect number— they symbolize that which has not yet reached completion.

Whether or not Mary fully realized that the old covenant was about to be fulfilled in the new, she courageously fostered the transition. Intervening in anticipation, she asked Jesus for an advance on the wine of the new covenant which, in her presence, would pour forth inexhaustibly at the hour of the cross.

"They have no wine." This was not simply an act of providential kindness to avoid embarrassment for the newlyweds; it was a cry of alarm that sought to avoid the death of the world.

Holy Mary, woman of the new wine, how many times have we too found that the banquet of life diminishes and happiness fades from the faces of those at table! We have no wine for the feast.

Even if the table lacks nothing else, without the wine, we lose our taste for bread. We eat listlessly, without real hunger The gourmet dishes of our cuisine have lost their old flavors; even exotic fruits now have little to offer us.

You know well the source of this insipidity. The reserves of meaning have drained out. Because we have no more wine, the tart aromas of crushed grapes have not delighted us for some time. In the wine cellar, the old barrels no longer ferment and the empty casks yield only dregs of vinegar.

Act out of compassion for us, then, and restore to us a joy for living. Only then will the jars of our existence brim over with ultimate meaning. The elation of living and of causing to live will bring us to dizzying heights.

Holy Mary, impatient promoter of change, at Cana in Galilee you prompted the greatest debut in history. At your request, the messianic wine of the new covenant began to flow. You remain for us the imperishable symbol of the superabundance of grace.

Obtain grace for us. Deliver us, we pray you, from easy gratification, from small "conversions" that don't cost, from comfortable solutions. Preserve us from the false securities of our closed areas, from never expanding our horizons, from unconditional trust in our plans.

When we begin to suspect that the new wine is bursting out of the old wineskins, give us the wisdom to replace the containers. When contentment with the "status quo" makes us too comfortable, inspire us with the resolve to pack up our encampment. If our energy flags, inflame our hearts with the courage to take new steps. Make us understand that closing ourselves off to the newness of the Spirit will stifle our spiritual growth.

Holy Mary, woman of the new wine, we thank you, because with the words: "Do whatever he tells you," you unveil for us the mysterious secret of youthfulness. You entrust to us the power to wake the dawn even in the depths of the night.

Chapter 17

WOMAN OF SILENCE

Among the many titles that the imagination of poets or the tenderness of popular piety have given to Mary, one has especially impressed me: Mary, cathedral of silence.

True, one can't always find silence in a metropolitan cathedral. But whoever goes in with the intention to pray can usually find a quiet corner. Sitting and looking, they can lift their gaze to the high vaulted ceiling to find the silence hidden above, in the shadow of the sweeping arches.

Mary is indeed like a Gothic cathedral that jealously cherishes silence. She does not break it even when she speaks. High above, silence plays in the many colored lights from the stained glass windows and with the inlay of the capitals and curves of the apse. The swell of the organ or the chanting of hymns from below do not break but exalt that silence.

Mary is a woman of silence because she measures her words. She speaks just four times in the Gospel: at the annunciation, when she visits Elizabeth and intones the *Magnificat*, when she finds Jesus in the temple, and at Cana in Galilee. Then, after telling the servants at the wedding to listen to the only word that counts, she keeps silence forever.

Yet, Mary's silence is not just the absence of voices or the lack of noise. It does not come from a sober asceticism. Rather, it is the theological covering of a presence, the shell around fullness, the womb cherishing the Word.

One of the last verses of the Letter to the Romans offers us an interpretive key to Mary's silence. It speaks of Jesus Christ as "the revelation of the mystery that was kept secret for long ages" (Rom 16:25). Christ is the mystery that was kept secret, kept hidden, literally wrapped in silence.

Silence surrounded the Word of God in the womb of eternity. Entering the womb of history, he could have no other covering but silence. Mary provided it with her own person. Thus, she prolonged on earth that hidden silence of heaven, showing us how to maintain the secrets of love. For all of us disturbed by noise, she has become the silent coffer of the Word: she "treasured all these things in her heart" (Lk 2:51).

Holy Mary, woman of silence, bring us to the sources of peace. Free us from the deluge of words, those of others, but especially our own. Children of noise, we think that our endless chatter can mask the insecurity that torments us. Help us understand that we can hear God speaking only when we grow quiet. Living with incessant noise, we think that we can dispel our fear by raising the volume on our televisions. Help us understand that God communicates with us only in silence, and that our din can silence his voice.

Explain to us the profound meaning of that text from Wisdom that fills us with wonder: "For while gentle silence enveloped all things, and night in its swift course was now half gone, your all-powerful word leaped from heaven, from the royal throne, into the midst of the land..." (Wis 18:14–15). Bring us, we pray you, to the dreamlike wonder of the first manger, and restore in our hearts nostalgia for that "silent night."

Holy Mary, woman of silence, tell us of your encounters with God. What fields did you go to on springtime afternoons, far from the bustle of Nazareth, to listen to his voice? What crevices of rock did you hide in as an adolescent, so that the violence of human noise would not profane your encounter with him?

What conversations did you hold with your girlfriends near the village fountain? What did you share with Joseph when he took you by the hand at dusk and headed out toward the plains of Esdraelon, or walked with you to the Lake of Tiberias on sunny days? Did you confide in him with words or with tears of happiness about the mystery concealed in your womb? Besides the spoken prayers and the patter of rain on the roof, what other voices resounded in the carpenter's workshop on winter evenings? Besides the treasure chest of your heart, did you also have a secret diary to which you entrusted Jesus' words? What did you talk about with each other for thirty years around your poor family table?

Holy Mary, admit us to your school. Keep us apart from the marketplace of noise where we risk becoming deaf. Keep us from an idle curiosity for unimportant news, which deafens us to the "Good News." Help us cherish the silence that restores to us an eagerness for contemplation even in the bustle of great cities. Help us to understand that the great things in life—conversion, love, sacrifice, and death—mature only in silence.

We wish to ask one last thing of you, dear Mother. Since you experienced the silence of God, as did Christ on the cross, do not leave our side at the hour of our trial. When the sun eclipses for us too, when heaven seems not to answer our cry, and the earth sounds hollow under our footsteps, stand by us so that the fear of abandonment will not make us despair. At that moment, break the silence and speak to us words of love! Then we will feel the thrill of Easter upon us, even before our agony finally ends.

Chapter 18

WOMAN OF OBEDIENCE

Sometimes we talk about "blind" obedience, but never about "deaf" obedience because the word "obey" derives from the Latin word meaning "to hear." When I discovered the origin of this term, I was also progressively freed from a wrong idea of obedience as the passive obliteration of my will. I then realized that obedience does not mean being weak-willed. Those who obey do not annul their freedom but exalt it. They do not waste their talents, but trade them in the logic of supply and demand. They do not abase themselves as if they were unthinking robots, but act on the basis of listening and dialogue.

The splendid phrase "to obey standing up" shows the authentic nature of obedience, which presupposes one who speaks and another who responds. One makes the proposal with respect, and the other complies out of love. One develops a plan without a trace of coercion, and the other cheerfully carries it out.

Indeed, one can obey only while standing up. By kneeling, one submits rather than obeys, gives in rather than loves, yields rather than collaborates. Obedience does not swallow an outrage, but experiences everything with freedom.

Obedience does not resign itself to silence in the face of vexations but gladly accepts a higher plan. Obedience does not mean keeping silent and being left with regrets. It responds with love; nevertheless, love requires courtesy rather than mastery in the one who requested.

Those who obey do not cease to will, but identify so much with the person they love that they align their wills with that of the other. Here we find the profound motive for Mary's obedience. She did not allow herself to be dispossessed of her will, not even by her Creator. But by saying "yes," she freely abandoned herself to him and entered the history of salvation with a responsible awareness. The angel Gabriel then returned to heaven and brought to the Lord an announcement no less joyful than the one he had brought down to earth.

Holy Mary, woman of surrender, you had the grace to "walk in the sight of the Lord"; help us, like you, to "seek his face." Help us understand that we can find peace only in his will. Even when he pushes us to leap into the darkness so that we might reach him, free us from the dizziness of the void. Give us the certainty that whoever obeys the Lord does not crash to the ground but falls into the loving arms of God.

Holy Mary, you know well that as long as we walk here below we can find God's face only in the many intermediary human faces we see, and that his words come to us only in the poor echoes of our earthly vocabulary. Give us the eyes of faith so that we might find God in all the events of daily life, through our dialogue with those persons whom he has chosen as a sign of his eternal will. Yet, preserve us also from complacency and the temptation to stay comfortably where we are, without trying to ascend to you.

Holy Mary, in order to save the life of your son, you eluded the order of a tyrannical dictator and fled to Egypt. At that moment, you became an icon of passive resistance. Teach us to be discerning people and give us the strength to counter injustice, to uphold the rights of the unborn, of children, of the poor…. May your wisdom inspire us to judge when we "must obey God rather than any human authority" (Acts 5:29). Allow us to invoke you in this way: "Holy Mary, woman who did not submit to injustice, pray for us."

Chapter 19

WOMAN OF SERVICE

This title might seem irreverent, possibly because it seems too poor a title to attribute to the Queen of angels and saints, or even because some might look down on those who perform manual labor.

Yet, Mary chose the above title herself. Twice in the Gospel of Luke, she defines herself as a servant. The first time she responded to the angel: "Here am I, the servant of the Lord" (Lk 1:38). The second time, she affirms in the *Magnificat* that God "has looked with favor on the lowliness of his servant" (Lk 1:48).

Mary is a woman of service, then, with full title. She bears this title by right of birth and seems to retain it jealously as an ancient coat-of-arms. Wasn't she, if not indeed a descendant of David as Joseph was, at least involved with "the house of David his servant"?

Through a kind of mirror image, this title helps her recognize the unmistakably similar traits in the elderly Simeon that lead her to place the child Jesus in the arms of that "servant" who could now finally go in peace. During the banquet at Cana, this title authorizes her to address "the servants" with those words, which, while demanding, invite all of us to do the same: "Do whatever he tells you."

This title would make the Blessed Virgin the protector of those who, through various roles—from tutor to babysitter, from nurse to household worker—provide domestic services. Although Mary applied this title to herself, it does not appear in the Litany of Loreto! Perhaps that is because even in the Church the idea of service evokes images of subjection, a drop in rank incompatible with the prestige of the position of Mother of God. This raises the suspicion that we don't take Mary's example seriously enough.

Holy Mary, servant of the Lord, you gave yourself to God body and soul, and entered his household as a family collaborator in his work of salvation. You are truly a servant whom grace has introduced into the intimacy of the Trinity and has made into a treasure chest of divine confidences. You are a servant of the kingdom and you gladly give service, knowing that it does not reduce your freedom but makes you participate in the lineage of God. We ask you to admit us to the school of that permanent ministry, which you teach in an incomparable way.

In contrast with you, we have trouble depending on God. We struggle to understand that only unconditional surrender to his sovereignty can make us see the value of every kind of human service. Trusting in the Lord's hands seems to us a game of chance. Instead of seeing submission to him in the context of a bilateral covenant, we feel it to be a kind of slavery. We are indeed jealous of our autonomy, so that even the solemn affirmation "to serve God is to reign" does not really convince us.

Holy Mary, servant of the Word, besides listening to it and keeping it, you accepted the Word incarnate in Christ. Help us to place Jesus at the center of our lives so that we might hear his secret suggestions. Enable us to be totally faithful to him. Give us the blessedness of those servants whom he will find still awake when he returns in the middle of the night, and for whom he will set the table and serve the food.

Make the Gospel the inspiring norm for all of our everyday choices. Keep us from the temptation of cutting corners on its demands. Help us to obey cheerfully. Finally, put wings on our feet so that we can carry out the missionary service of proclaiming the Word to the farthest reaches of the earth.

Holy Mary, servant of the world, immediately after declaring yourself the servant of God you hastened to become Elizabeth's handmaid. Give us the urgency that guided your steps. Help us to serve selflessly not out of self-interest, and may the shadow of power never lengthen over our offerings.

You experienced the tribulations of the poor, help us to place our lives at the service of others with hidden deeds performed in silence. Make us aware that the King disguises himself in the weary and the oppressed. Open our hearts to the sufferings of our brothers and sisters. So that we can intuit their needs, give us eyes filled with tenderness and hope—the eyes you had that day at Cana in Galilee.

Chapter 20

TRUE WOMAN

I confess that it disturbs me when I think of Mary (that incredible dream dreamed by the Lord), and then watch the tears of Palestinian mothers on television, or the undernourished faces of women in the Amazon, or the subhuman conditions of girls in Bangladesh. I cannot help wondering if Mary's story has anything to do with these suffering women. When I see a prostitute on the street whose misery has driven her to sell herself in order to survive, I wonder if Mary would walk straight ahead, as I do. And yet, I can hardly imagine what Mary would say to her if she *did* stop.

So, every time I listen to the pain of so many women abused by men or deprived of their most elementary rights by male injustice, I make a great effort to see the connection between them and Mary. And when I think about professional women, this same problem with their connection to Mary insistently comes back. Is there an actress in a show or a soprano at an opera who invokes Mary's name before an appearance? Do the photo models on magazine covers or the skating champions at sports events ever contemplate Mary's supernatural charm? What do female flight attendants or ballerinas of famous companies think about her? Apart from wearing medals of Mary around their neck, how does the name of Mary affect the lives of women?

Is Mary only a point of reference for cloistered nuns and pious girls, or does she voice the aspirations of every woman who wants to live femininity to its fullest? Do women look upon Mary with tenderness because her earthly life sums up the sorrowful mysteries of all forms of their suffering? Is she only an eloquent symbol of the joyful mysteries of experiencing an exodus from the "bitter waters" of servitude? Or is she the image that synthesizes the glorious mysteries of woman's definitive liberation from every type of slavery that, throughout history, has robbed her of dignity? I cannot answer these questions, which may strike some as being foolish, but I can offer a prayer over them.

Holy Mary, true woman, icon of women humiliated in the land of Egypt, subjected to the cruelties of the pharaohs of all ages, we pray to you for all the women on earth. Since the time on Calvary when suffering pierced your soul, you have understood the lament of every mother; you know the loneliness of every widow; you feel the humiliation of every woman who suffers abasement.

While the soldiers despoiled Jesus of his garments, grief despoiled you of your titles. You appeared simply as a woman, to the point that your dying only-begotten Son could call you by no other name: "Woman, here is your son" (Jn 19:26). You who remained standing at the foot of the cross, help all women who feel overwhelmed with every kind of suffering. May they take inspiration from your feminine dignity.

Holy Mary, icon of the feminine world which has set out on the roads of exodus, help women who make this laborious journey so that they do not wander aimlessly in the desert. Help them to find the right paths so that your image as a truly successful woman might shine for all women, like the luminous cloud in the desert.

Holy Mary, icon of the feminine world at last established in the Promised Land, help us to read history and interpret life with feminine tenderness and strength. You are the image not only of the new woman but also of the new humanity preserved from the mirages of false liberation. Help us to thank God for showing us, in you, what it means to be a true woman.

Chapter 21

WOMAN OF THE PEOPLE

The Lord chose Mary from among the people. He found Mary in the maze of alleys, fragrant with the aroma of midday soup, and cheered by the shouts of fruit vendors. She was chosen from among the young women who stood on staircase landings packed with flowers and speaking of love. From among her neighbors in the courtyard prolonging the evening's stories until the last yawn, before the oil in the lamp burned out and keys clanked in the locks and bolts secured the doors, Mary was chosen.

He discovered her there. He didn't find her along the avenues of the capital but in a village of shepherds, unknown in the Hebrew scriptures. The inhabitants of nearby villages even spoke of it with sarcasm: "...Can anything good come out of Nazareth?" (Jn 1:46).

God discovered her there, in the midst of common people, and he made Mary his. She did not possess any special dynastic ancestry. The heraldry of her family did not boast of noble crests like Joseph's. Although he worked as a carpenter, he sprang from the illustrious house of David. Mary, however, was a woman of the people. She absorbed her peoples' language and culture, the refrains of their songs and the secrecy of their lament, the custom of silence and the stigma of poverty.

Before becoming a mother, Mary was a daughter of the people. She belonged to the *anawim*, the ranks of the poor; she belonged to the remnant of Israel, which had survived the devastation of national tragedies. She belonged to that nucleus which kept alive the promises to the patriarchs and the hopes of the prophets, as Zephaniah prophesied: "For I will leave in the midst of you a people humble and lowly. They shall seek refuge in the name of the Lord—the remnant of Israel" (Zeph 3:12–13).

A woman of the people, Mary mingled with the pilgrims going up to the temple and accompanied their psalm singing. If on one of these journeys she lost the twelve-year-old Jesus, it was because, "assuming that he was in the group of travelers" (Lk 2:44), she knew her son understood the ways of the common people.

The Gospel of Mark has an incomparably beautiful icon, which portrays Mary's nature, vocation, and destiny among her people. One day, while Jesus was speaking to the crowd seated around him in a circle, Mary arrived with some relatives. When someone told Jesus they were there, he pointed to the crowd and exclaimed, "Here is my mother...." At first glance, that seems like a discourtesy. Rather, Jesus' reply, which identifies his mother with the crowd, is the most splendid monument to Mary, a woman of the people.

Holy Mary, woman of the people, thank you for sharing life with the people, both before and after the angel's annunciation, and for not asking Gabriel to stand guard at your house. Thank you because, while being the Mother of God, you did not with-draw into the dwelling of your spiritual aristocracy, but experienced the poverty and longing of all the women in Nazareth.

Thank you, because in the summer you joined the women who gleaned in the sun-baked fields. On winter days, when thunder rumbled over the hills of Galilee, you took refuge in your neighbors' houses. On the Sabbath, to praise the Lord, you par-ticipated with your friends at the synagogue service. When death visited your village, you drenched your handkerchief with tears. On feast days, when a wed-ding procession passed by, you too waited on the street, standing on tiptoe to see the bride and groom.

Holy Mary, we need you today more than ever. In our difficult times, the common good often takes second place to special interests, with factions re-placing solidarity. The party prevails over the public good, the association over the nation.

Give us a greater awareness of being a people. We believers, who call ourselves the people of God, feel the duty to offer a strong witness of communion. You, "the great pride of our nation" (Jud 15:9), stay at our side in this difficult undertaking.

Holy Mary, teach us to share with all people the joys and the hopes, the sorrows and the grief that have marked the path of our civilization. Give us the desire to stand in the middle, as you did in the Cenacle. Free us from self-sufficiency and bring us out of our caves of isolation.

You, who are invoked in the *favelas* of Latin America and in the skyscrapers of New York, give justice to peoples destroyed by misery, give inner peace to peoples wearied with riches. Restore to them the true meaning of living, so that they might sing together at last psalms of liberty.

Chapter 22

WOMAN WHO DANCES

Recently I read a book on Mary written by a renowned teacher of anthropology. Toward the end of the book I came to a sentence that seemed to me a grave insult: "Mary could never dance." This statement annoyed me immensely. I thought it was an awful disregard and outrage against Mary's humanity. It denigrates that which makes Mary dear to us, what she holds in common with the children of Eve.

Indeed, what is hidden behind the author's statement if not an affirmation that Mary did not have a body like other women? Does it not imply that Mary's femininity was so disincarnate and evanescent as to make it impossible for her to dance? Does it not seem like a blasphemy even to suggest that

Mary was a creature drained of passions, poor in impulse, lacking in human warmth, enfeebled by fasting and abstinence, kneeling on the cold mirrors of contemplation, incapable of those inner longings that explode into song and dance?

One word we find on Mary's lips in the Gospel shows she was skilled in dancing: "to exult." It comes from the Latin *ex-saltare*, which means to leap for joy. Thus, when Mary exclaims, *"My spirit exults in God, my savior,"* she not only reveals her extraordinary musical competence but also makes us wonder if she sang her *Magnificat* while dancing.

I emphasize this particular "artistic" aspect of Mary because of the connection between dancing and death. How does death connect with dancing? Perhaps the image of "dancing with death" helps to bring out my meaning. To say that Mary could never dance means she is a stranger to what death and dance have in common: shortness of breath, the spasm of agony, the painful contraction of the body. It empties Our Lady's suffering of any salvific value and reduces the mystery of the Mother of Sorrows—despite the seven swords that pierced her heart—to a hollow spectacle. It strikes Mary from the scenario of Good Friday, in which she is a protagonist along-side Jesus, and the drama of redemption reaches its decisive moments.

Holy Mary, woman who knows well how to dance and is well acquainted with suffering, help us under-stand that suffering is not our final shore. We must, however, pass through it to set down our baggage! We dare not ask to be spared from suffering and grief. We only pray that, at the moment of our trial, you preserve us from the lament of despair.

Holy Mary, we ask you to stay near us at the hour of our death because we know that you have truly experienced the pain of death—not so much your own, but the violent death of your Son.

We beg you, at the last moment, to show us the tenderness you felt for Jesus, when "from noon on, darkness came over the whole land until three in the afternoon" (Mt 27:45). In those dark hours, shaken only by the death rattle of the condemned, perhaps you danced your laments as a mother around the cross, pleading for the return of the sun.

Then, holy woman of the total eclipse, repeat that dance around the crosses of your children. If you are there, the light will soon break through. Then the most tragic gibbet will flower like a tree in springtime.

Holy Mary, make us understand that the feast is our ultimate vocation. Increase, then, our reserves of courage, double our provisions of love, and fuel for us our lamps of hope. When our lives lack love, help us to await your Son with faith so that we can say to him: "You have turned my mourning into dancing; you have taken off my sackcloth and clothed me with joy" (Ps 30:11).

Chapter 23

WOMAN OF HOLY SATURDAY

Some moments hold so much mystery that they seem to bring the past back to life. Other moments hold so much promise that they seem to anticipate future bliss. Holy Saturday possesses many such moments. In it the dams confining the present suddenly rupture and the soul reaches back into the recesses of its memory, or else reaches forward to touch the shores of the eternal and steal a taste of its secrets.

How can we explain the special atmosphere that pervades Holy Saturday if not by this looking back into the past? From the first greetings of "Happy Easter," it dissolves into a thousand rivulets of memory, flowing through the rituals of preparing for Easter. The friend arrives to visit after so many years and brings traces of a shared childhood. The expensive gift waits in the kitchen, not far from the Easter bread and colored eggs. The empty womb of the church beckons with a silence overflowing with reproof. Finally, in the evening one enters to be reconciled with God and feel lost innocence restored.

How can we explain that pervasive sentiment of peace, which on Holy Saturday, at least fleetingly, breaks in from the future and calls upon us with strange questions that we now feel we can answer gladly? Will people always exchange handshakes and smiles as they are doing today? Will days come that do not know the sorrow of tears? Will we still give of ourselves when we no longer wear our festive garments? The strange charm of Holy Saturday touches the soul with feelings of solidarity and makes us look to a future of hope!

What will the trees do tonight when the alleluias sound forth? Will the animals of the forest howl their concerts while the Church sings the *Exsultet?* How will the sea, breaking on the reefs, react to the news of the resurrection? Beyond the gates of the cemetery, will the tombs of the dead tremble under the full moon? Will the mountains, unseen by anyone, dance with joy around the valleys?

On Holy Saturday, the present seems to oscillate between the past and the future because the absolute and most silent protagonist of this day is Mary. After the burial of Jesus, she kept faith in Jesus alive on earth. Although the wind of Golgotha had blown out all the lamps, hers still burned brightly—only hers. Throughout Holy Saturday, Mary remains the only point of light, a beacon for the blazes of the past and the fires of the future. On this day, she wanders through the roads of the earth with her light in her hands. When she lifts it toward one slope, she evokes memories of holiness from the night of the ages; when she lifts it toward another, she anticipates echoes of future transfigurations from the eternal mansions.

Holy Mary, woman of Holy Saturday in whom, for at least one day, the faith of the whole Church is gathered, you are the final point of contact with heaven, preserving the earth from the tragic black-out of grace. Lead us by the hand to the threshold of the light, which emanates from Easter as its supreme source.

Retain in our spirit the best portions of our memories, so that in the fragments of the past we might recover the best part of ourselves. Stir up in our hearts, through the signs of the future, an intense desire for renewal and a hopeful commitment to go on through history.

Holy Mary, help us understand that all of life, suspended between the mists of Good Friday and the expectations of Easter Sunday, resembles this day so much. It dawns as the day of hope when we cleanse the linens soaked in tears and blood and dry them in the spring sunshine so they might become altar cloths.

Tell us again, then, that a person is always taken down from every cross. Every human bitterness dissolves into a smile; every sin finds redemption, and even mourning garments change into vestments of joy. Help us understand that the most tragic rhapsodies lead to the first steps of the dance, and funeral

hymns already contain the festive motifs of the paschal alleluia.

Holy Mary, woman of Holy Saturday, at the twilight of this day, tell us how you prepared yourself
to meet your risen Son. What tunic did you put on?
What sandals did you wear so as to run more speed-
ily over the grass? How did you braid your long
hair? What words of love did you go on repeating
secretly, so as to tell him all at once as soon as he
appeared to you?

Sweetest Mother, prepare us also for our meeting
with him. Stir up a devout impatience within us for
his return on Sunday. Dress us in wedding garments. Come close to us and let us practice our songs
as we wait, for here time never passes.

Chapter 24

WOMAN OF THE THIRD DAY

Although the Gospel speaks of Jesus appearing on Easter day to many people, such as Mary Magdalene, the other devout women, and the disciples, it tells us nothing about any appearance of the risen Son to his Mother. I like to think that Jesus did not need to appear to Mary because she alone was present at the resurrection.

Theologians tell us that the resurrection was hidden from everyone's eyes; it unfolded in the unfathomable depths of mystery and, in its historical occurrence, had no witness. However, I believe Mary was an exception—she alone must have been present at this supreme turning point in human history.

124

She alone was present at the Incarnation of the Word. At his birth from her virginal womb of flesh, she became the first woman to look upon God made man. So I think she alone must have been present at his departure from the virginal womb of stone, the sepulcher where no one had ever been buried (cf. Jn 19:41). Thus, she became the first woman to look upon her glorified Son.

The others witnessed the appearance of the Risen One; Mary witnessed the resurrection. Moreover, the bond between Mary and Jesus was so close that they shared every redeeming experience; this leads me to think that the resurrection, the peak moment of redemption, would have found her united with her Son. If she hadn't been, it would seem a strangely unjustified absence.

To confirm for us, however, Mary's profound link to her Son's Passover, in two places the Gospel uses the phrase "the third day" in connection with Mary. This phrase can be seen as an allusion to the resurrection. St. Luke uses it when he narrates the disappearance of the twelve-year-old Jesus in the temple and his rediscovery on the "third day." Some scholars interpret this episode as a veiled prophecy of what would happen at a Passover many years later in Jerusalem, when Jesus completed his passage from this world to the Father. The loss of the child Jesus appears as a parable alluding to the disappearance of the adult Jesus behind the stone of the tomb, and to his glorious reappearance after three days.

St. John refers to the "third day" in the passage about the wedding at Cana. Mary's intervention, anticipating Jesus' "hour," introduces to the human banquet the wine of the new Paschal covenant, and makes the "glory" of his resurrection burst forth ahead of time. John introduces this episode with the deliberate phrase: "the third day." Mary, then, is so involved with the "third day" that she is not only the firstborn daughter of Easter, but in a certain sense she is also its mother.

Holy Mary, woman of the third day, wake us from the sleep of the rock. Come to bring us the news that Easter dawns for us in the heart of the night as well. Do not wait for the first light of the sun. Do not wait until the women come with their ointments. Come yourself first; as your eyes reflect the Risen One, let us hear your direct testimony.

When the other women arrive in the garden—their feet wet with dew—let them find us already awake, knowing that you came to us first, the only witness of the duel between Life and Death. Although we have confidence in their words, we feel death's tentacles so close that we need more than their testimony. They indeed have seen the Victor's triumph, yet they did not see the adversary's defeat. Only you can assure us that death has truly been killed, because you saw it lifeless on the ground.

Holy Mary, give us the certainty that, despite everything, death can no longer hold onto us. Help us believe that injustice will sink into defeat, that the blaze of war will flicker out, that the sufferings of the poor will end. Help us eradicate hunger, racism, and drug abuse, so that the tears of all victims of violence and pain will dry up like dew in the springtime sun.

Holy Mary, pull away the burial cloth of despair from our face and fold up the shroud of our sins. Despite the lack of work, housing, and bread, comfort us with the new wine of joy and with the unleavened Easter bread of solidarity.

Give us peace and keep us from selfishness. Bestow on us the hope that, when the moment of the decisive challenge comes for us, you will be the arbiter who, on the third day, will at last confirm our victory.

Chapter 25

WOMAN OF THE BANQUET

This title relates to the unique definition that a medieval writer, Ildephonse of Toledo, gives for the Blessed Virgin: *totius Trinitatis nobile triclinium*, which means "the noble banquet table for the three divine Persons." This splendid and bold image places Our Lady in relation to the Trinity. It compares Mary to an elegant table around which the Father, the Son, and the Spirit express their conviviality.

Such an image reminds one of the famous icon of Rublev. At its center, this image depicts a table, which brings the three Persons together in solidarity of life and communion of works. Ildephonse's title suggests that Mary is precisely that noble "table."

Let us stop here. We would not want to get lost in a terrain full of doctrinal snares even for the cleverest theologians. It is enough to have intuited that Mary has a fundamental relationship to the Trinity.

Although it is difficult to speculate on Mary's relation to the divine community living in heaven, it is easier to discern her function within every human community living here on earth.

We know this from the family to the parish, from the religious institute to the diocese, from the prayer group to the seminary…. Every group that wants to live in the light of the Gospel carries within itself something sacramental. By its nature, it is a sign and instrument of the Trinitarian communion. It should replicate the logic of the Trinity, live out its communion, and express its mystery. We could define ecclesial communities as scale models of that mysterious experience which the Father, the Son, and the Holy Spirit live in heaven.

In heaven, three equal and distinct Persons live their communion to such a degree that they are one God. On earth, many equal and distinct persons ought to live their communion so as to form one single body: the body of Christ.

Every ecclesial group has the task of presenting itself as an icon of the Trinity. Such a community recognizes the faces of its members, fosters equality, and allows each one to retain their unique identity.

If Mary is the noble "table" around which the three divine Persons sit, we can imagine how important is the role she plays in those earthly communities that reflect the Trinitarian communion. Is it too daring to think that without this "noble banquet table" of the Virgin, around whom we are called to sit, every attempt at communion will fail?

Holy Mary, woman of the banquet, you remind us of family banquets of an earlier time when our earthly mothers sat at table. They cherished each one of us with their eyes and, without words, would tearfully plead with us to agree among ourselves and to love one another. They worried if anyone was missing, and would finally relax only when the last family member reached home.... Mary, perhaps only in heaven will we discover how important you are in the growth of our human communion.

This is true especially in the Church. Yes, the Church is built around the Eucharist. But you are the table around which the family gathers to hear the Word of God and share the bread of heaven— just as in the icon of Rublev. Help us experience your motherly presence gathering us together.

Holy Mary, nourish in our local churches the desire for communion. They should bring into the world the desire and the impetus for Trinitarian communion, like so many Eucharistic particles scattered over the earth. Help them to overcome their disagreements. Intervene whenever discord rises in their hearts. Extinguish the hotbeds of factions and settle their conflicts.

Holy Mary, look upon all families in difficulty. So many victims of the hurricanes caused by our modern times have suffered shipwreck and are adrift. Heal marriages that are in trouble and call spouses together to the table. Reanimate their old love, renew their earlier dreams, rekindle their lost hopes, and help them understand that they can still start afresh.

Finally, we pray to you for all the peoples of the earth, wounded by hate and divided by prejudice. Awaken in them a desire to sit at one table so that, with greed consumed and rumors of war extinguished, they might eat the bread of justice together in peace. While different in language, race, and culture, they will come back to live in harmony by sitting around you. Then your motherly eyes, witnessing here on earth to that image of the Trinitarian communion in heaven, will shine with joy.

Chapter 26

WOMAN OF THE UPPER ROOM

The term "icon" refers to the sacred images painted on wood, which Eastern Christians venerate with special devotion. Bathed in light, these images hold a spark of the divine mystery and on that account, someone has defined them as windows in time opening into eternity. The term "icon" is also used today to speak of those biblical scenes that bear an important message of salvation. Perhaps because of the brilliant images they convey these scenes resemble commemorative medallions.

The first chapter of the Acts of the Apostles contains an icon of extraordinary splendor. It says that after the ascension, while the apostles were awaiting the Holy Spirit, they "went to the room upstairs

where they were staying…. All these were constantly devoting themselves to prayer, together with
certain women, including Mary the mother of Jesus"
(Acts 1:13–14).

Acts thus portrays the last biblical scene in which
Our Lady appears before she withdrew definitively
from the footlights. Mary appears in the upper room,
almost as if to indicate the spiritual levels at which
the existence of every Christian should unfold.
Mary's whole life developed, as it were, at a high
altitude.

But she never scorned the homes of poor people.
Quite the contrary. She lived among ordinary people.
The shepherds' wives may have bartered some of
their wool or cheese for a loaf of the bread she had
baked. Mary's neighbors never realized the mystery
hidden in that apparently common life. Nor did the
countrywomen of Nazareth notice in her an aloof-
ness that might indicate that she thought of herself
as superior. She went with them to the market and
negotiated prices as they did. She went out with the
others to the street, after summer rains, to dam up

the torrents of water. On spring evenings her voice, which never stood out over others, resounded in the courtyard as part of the choir singing ancient songs.

Although aware of her supernatural destiny, Mary never wanted to live apart. She never built a pedestal of glory for herself, but felt the joy of living with ordinary people. She did, however, reserve an observatory at the highest level, from where she contemplated not only the ultimate meaning of her human activity, but also the immense extent of God's kindness.

Two strategic points in Mary's life confirm that she habitually dwelled in that upper room the Holy Spirit had called her to inhabit: the loftiness of the *Magnificat* and the altar of Golgotha. From the height of the *Magnificat* she cast her gaze to the farthest limits of time: "from now on all generations will call me blessed" (Lk 1:48). Perceiving that God's mercy stretches "from generation to generation," she provides the most insightful reading known of the history of salvation.

From the altar of Golgotha she cast her gaze to

the far limits of space. Clasping the world in a single embrace, she offers us the surest guarantee that the Spirit, sent forth by the last breath of the dying Christ, will reach all the corners of the earth now seen by her maternal eyes.

Holy Mary, woman of the upper room, splendid icon of the Church, you experienced your personal Pentecost at the annunciation, when the Holy Spirit came upon you and the power of the Most High overshadowed you. You stayed at the Cenacle to pray with those around you, that they might receive the same gift you had been graced with at Nazareth. The Church, too, now enriched by the outpouring of the Spirit, has the duty to pray for the outpouring of God on every area of the world.

Give the Church the elation of the heights, the measure of long times, the logic of comprehensive judgments. Give her your farsightedness. Let her look upon history from the observation posts of the kingdom. For only if she can train her eye from the highest observation point, where the panoramas spread the farthest, can she assist the Spirit in renewing the face of the earth.

Holy Mary, help the Church's pastors to dwell in those high regions of the spirit, where it is easier to forgive human weakness, to judge with greater understanding, and to more firmly trust in the hope of the resurrection. Invite them to rise to the heights with you, because only from certain vantage points can one's gaze truly reach to the far corners of the earth and measure the vastness of the waters over which the Holy Spirit hovers.

Holy Mary, let us contemplate through your windows the joyful, sorrowful, and glorious mysteries of life—joy, victory, health, illness, pain, death.... Only from that height will success not cause giddiness, and only at that level will defeat not plunge us into the void.

Facing outward from your window, the fresh wind of the Spirit will blow upon us more easily with the exultation of his seven gifts. Wisdom will fill our days, and we will understand where the paths of life go. We will take counsel over the most practical courses, and decide to face them with fortitude. The snares hidden by the road won't entrap us when we perceive the nearness of God alongside those who walk devoutly. We will go forth joyfully in holy fear of him, and thus hasten, as you did, the coming of Pentecost to the world.

138

Chapter 27
MOST BEAUTIFUL WOMAN

The Gospel says nothing about Mary's face, or even about Jesus' face, for that matter. However, I think that Mary must have been most beautiful, and I don't mean only her soul. Certainly, with no shadow of sin, her soul was so pure that God could see his reflection within it, like the Alpine Mountains reflected on shining lakes. But I am also speaking about Mary's physical beauty, something theology seems to pass over even while it accepts poetic celebrations of her beauty: "Beautiful Virgin, clothed with the sun, crowned with stars, you pleased the supreme sun so much that he concealed his light within you...." It is mirrored in the songs of the humble: "Look upon your people, lovely lady..." and in the passionate refrains of the faithful: "At dawn you rise so beautiful...there is no star more beautiful than you." Even the liturgical allusions in the *Tota pulchra* speak of her beauty: "You are all beautiful, Mary." You are splendid in soul and in body!

Theology, however, goes no further; it does not lose its balance. It remains silent about Mary's human beauty perhaps out of modesty or perhaps because it has spent itself speculating on her supernatural charm. Even today, theology is burdened with an unresolved diffidence concerning the salvific function of the body.

Still, it should not be difficult to find in the Gospel a revealing hint of Mary's corporeal beauty. Luke uses an important Greek word laden with a mysterious significance not yet entirely explained. This word, which substantially establishes the whole series of supernatural privileges of the girl of Nazareth, resounds in the angel's greeting: *kécharitôménê*. Difficult to translate, the term is sometimes rendered as "full of grace." But could it not also find an equivalent in "most graceful," with evident allusions to the enchanting splendor of her human face as well? I think so, and without straining the word's meaning. Similarly, in a noted discourse to the International Mariological Congress (May 16, 1975), Pope Paul VI dared to speak for the first time about Mary as "the woman clothed with the sun, in whom the purest rays of human beauty mingle with the superhuman yet accessible ones of supernatural beauty."

Holy Mary, most beautiful woman, through you we thank the Lord for the mystery of beauty. He has scattered it throughout the earth so that an irrepressible desire for heaven might be kept alive in our wayfarer's hearts.

He makes it shine in the majesty of snowcapped peaks, in the hushed silence of the forests, in the raging power of the sea, in the perfumed rustle of grass on quiet evenings. This gift elates us because, if only for a moment, it offers us fleeting peepholes to glance upon the eternal.

142

He makes it shine in the tears of a baby, in the harmony of the human body, in a child's dancing eyes, in the white tremor of the aged, in the silence of a canoe gliding on the river, in the brilliant colors worn by marathon runners in early spring. Yet, this gift can also make us despair—we bet and lose this wealth at the gambling table of time.

Holy Mary, splendid as a full moon in spring, let us be reconciled with your beauty. Help us, we pray you, to understand the dignity of the human body, which reflects the person. Give us a heart as pure as yours. Help us to appreciate the beautiful things of life, knowing that they reflect the beauty of the Creator.

Holy Mary, most beautiful woman, help us understand that beauty will save the world. The power of law, the wisdom of the learned, and the cleverness of diplomacy are not enough to preserve the earth from catastrophe. Today, unfortunately, when values are adrift, even the old buoys that once offered a stable anchor to vessels in danger are themselves in danger of sinking.

In this dark chamber of reason, there shines another light, which can make an imprint on the film of good sense: the light of beauty. For this reason, Holy Virgin Mary, we want to feel the beauty of your human splendor, just as we feel the sometimes deceptive allure of earthly creatures. Already the contemplation of your holiness helps us to keep on the right course. To know that you are most beautiful in body as well as in soul gives us a motive for unbelievable hope. It helps us grasp that all earthly beauty is just a seed destined to flower in the green fields above.

Chapter 28

ELEGANT WOMAN

The Gospel says nothing about Mary's elegance, yet some biblical verses seem to allude to it. We can recall that text from the Song of Songs in which the liturgy perceives the figure of the woman who fights on our behalf against the forces of evil: "Who is this that looks forth like the dawn, fair as the moon, bright as the sun, terrible as an army with banners?" (6:10).

The Latin text says *"Electa ut sol."* *Electa* means elegant; both words have the same root. Elegant as the sun!

The Book of Revelation also speaks of the cosmic elements of the sun, the moon, and the stars. Artists of every century have used these symbols to portray Mary's beauty: "A great portent appeared in heaven: a woman clothed with the sun, with the moon under her feet, and on her head a crown of twelve stars" (Rev 12:1).

Another noted text follows soon after: "…for the marriage of the Lamb has come, and his bride has made herself ready; to her it has been granted to be clothed with fine linen, bright and pure" (Rev 19:7–8). Although this text refers to the New Jerusalem, tradition has accommodated it to Mary through that play of theological blending by which reality and signs often switch places.

The Virgin, this marvelous anticipation of the Church, descends from heaven adorned with jewels and draped with veils, ready as a bride adorned for her bridegroom. All of it is a hymn to Mary's elegance.

Clearly, this elegance flows from Mary's interior refinement, and when we attentively meditate on the Gospel, allusions to Mary's physical elegance do not seem totally out of place.

Perhaps in the intimacy of their home, Jesus might have enjoyed bestowing on his mother the names of the most perfumed plants, as the Church would come to do: rose of Sharon, lily of the valley, cedar of Lebanon, palm of Kadesh.... Perhaps Jesus was thinking specifically of her, the flower of beauty, when he said to the crowd: "Consider the lilies of the field, how they grow; they neither toil nor spin, yet I tell you, even Solomon in all his glory was not clothed like one of these" (Mt 6:28–29).

Perhaps he was also thinking of her when he said: "The eye is the lamp of the body. So, if your eye is healthy, your whole body will be full of light" (Mt 6:22). In that moment the memory of his mother's eyes may have flashed before him, eyes that revealed the transparency of her soul and gave the depth of holiness even to the elegance of her body.

Holy Mary, elegant woman, give us your apparel, acquaint us with your tastes. You know well that we are referring to those interior "garments" which adorned your earthly existence: gratitude, simplicity, kind words, transparency, tenderness, and wonder. Though the world may believe so, these garments have not gone out of fashion. Even if we can't quite fit into them, we will adapt them to our size.

Reveal to us, we pray, the secret of your beauty. Keep us from those lapses of "style" that often reveal our vulgarity. Help us discover in the splendor of nature and art the signs of God's elegance.

Holy Mary, free us from the coarse spirit we carry within, despite the fine clothing that we wear. How far we are from your spiritual elegance! We may wear stylish clothes, but we fail in our human relationships. We may wear expensive perfume, but we also wear a scowl. We freshen our breath with mouthwash and then speak cutting words.

Obtain for us the grace to compensate for our excesses. Help us to see in every person a face to discover, contemplate, and cherish. Holy Mary, you grasped with such attention the presence of God in your life, help us also to detect his passing. Only rarely does he break into our history with the power of hurricanes, earthquakes, or fires; rather, as on Mount Horeb, he makes himself heard in the slightest stirring of the leaves (cf. 1 Kgs 19:8–13). We need delicate antennae to detect his whisper. We need a sensitive ear to hear the rustle of his steps when, at midday—as with Adam—he comes down to our garden.

Help us discern God's delicacy in that biblical verse when the Lord almost expresses shyness about disturbing us: "Listen! I am standing at the door, knocking; if you hear my voice and open the door, I will come in to you and eat with you, and you with me" (Rev 3:20). Make us prompt to answer his discreet knock. Let us open the door to him right away, make a feast with him, and lead him to table with us.

Chapter 29

WOMAN OF OUR TIME

We like to see Mary at home, speaking our language, knowledgeable in both old traditions and popular customs. By connecting two or three names, she reconstructs your family tree, showing that you are related to practically the whole city. We want to imagine her like this—immersed in the town news, wearing modern clothes, shopping in the same supermarket, earning her bread like everybody else, parking her car next to ours. Mary is a woman of all ages, with whom all the sons and daughters of Eve, in whatever phase of life, can feel close.

We want to imagine her as an adolescent, coming back from the beach in shorts, her eyes reflecting the green ocean. In winter, carrying her knapsack, she too is going to the skating rink. Walking along the street, she greets people kindly. In anyone who looks at her, she inspires a sense of chastity. In the evening she talks with her friends on Main Street, making them happy.

We want to give her one of our surnames and think of her as a student at our high school, or as a worker at a factory in our city, or as a computer programmer in the software company across the street, or as a clerk in a boutique.

We want to meet her as she walks through the streets of an historic downtown and stops to talk with a woman selling flowers. We want to find her in the cemetery on Sunday as she brings a bouquet for her deceased, or when she goes shopping on Thursday and checks out prices. At midday, with all the other mothers in front of the school, she waits for her child to come out, then brings him home and covers him with kisses.

We don't want her to be a guest but a fellow citizen, privy to our community's problems, yet also happy to share our spiritual experience, contradictory and exultant. We want Mary to be proud of the cultural richness of our city, of its churches, its art, its music, its history, and to be glad to belong to our people.

We want to see Mary listed in our phone books. She is always ready to give us a hand, to share her hope with us. With her impressive purity, she makes us feel our need for God. We want her to share with us moments of celebration and of tears, work in the office and at home, aromas of oven and laundry, tears of departures and arrivals.

Holy Mary, woman of our time, come to live in our midst. You foretold that all generations would call you blessed. Our generation too wants to sing your praises, not only for the great things the Lord has done for you in the past, but also for the wonders he continues to work in you today.

Help us feel your closeness to our problems. Holy Mary, free us from the danger of thinking that the spiritual experiences you lived two thousand years ago have no bearing on us today, children of a postmodern civilization which often regards itself as post-Christian.

152

Make us understand that modesty, humility, and purity bear fruit in every season of history, and that time has not altered certain values such as selflessness, obedience, trust, tenderness, and forgiveness. These values still hold and will never fall into disuse. Come, then, into our midst and teach us those human virtues you practiced so well.

Holy Mary, when Jesus gave you to us as our mother, he made you our contemporary. Come to our side and listen to us as we confide in you the everyday anxieties that assail our modern life: low income, stress, an uncertain future, doubts, fears, loneliness, fractured relationships, lack of love and communication even with those dearest to us, the dullness of sin.... Make us feel your reassuring presence, so we will know that you always stand by our side.

Chapter 30

WOMAN OF THE FINAL HOUR

"Now and at the hour of our death."

I think it sounds better in Latin, especially when sung: *Nunc et in hora mortis nostrae.* Then it seems that the rhythmic chant of the prayer condenses the most agonizing supplications of the human heart into those last words: *"Now and at the hour of our death."*

The Hail Mary might seem monotonous to some people. But clusters of intense feelings leap out from those few words and leave one wondering if they are pushing one toward the line separating time from eternity. Or are they drawing one back into a remote past laden with memories?

As we repeat these words, tender images fill the mind. We remember our human mothers, who on winter evenings, or under the stars on summer nights, surrounded by family members and neighbors, repeated with the rosary in hand: "Holy Mary, Mother of God...."

It seems we always ask Mary for the same thing: "Pray for us sinners." Perhaps this is because it basically sums up our essential plea. Everything else flows from this demand, and after which, fifty times over, comes the same touching plea: "Now and at the hour of our death."

How did the Hail Mary come to distill the essence of our supplications into one request? I can suggest two possible reasons.

Above all, Mary is an expert of that hour, because she was present at the hour of the Son. She lived it as a protagonist in the supreme drama of death and glorification, which the whole history of salvation tends toward. In that hour, Jesus handed over to her all his brothers and sisters symbolized by John, so that Mary might consider them as her children.

From that moment on, she became the guardian of *our* final hour. She makes herself present in that fraction of time in which each of us finally decides his or her eternal destiny.

The second reason is that we find it difficult to pass through the hour of death. This transition frightens us because it bears the greatest unknown. Death disturbs us because we cannot predetermine its time, place, or modality. It is like walking across a narrow rope bridge swaying in the wind over a deep canyon. Hence, the realism of the prayer: "Pray for us...now and at the hour of our death."

Holy Mary, woman of the final hour, help each of us when death strikes on the clock of our life, so that we might face it as serenely as St. Francis of Assisi: "Praise to you, my Lord, for our sister, bodily death, from whom no living person may escape."

Holy Mary, woman of the final hour, when the great evening comes for us and the sun sinks into twilight, come to our side to help us face the night.

You have already experienced this with Jesus when, at his death, the sun was eclipsed and a great darkness fell over the whole earth. Stay with us too when we die. Place yourself under our cross and watch over us at our hour of darkness. Free us from the terror of the abyss. Even in the eclipse, give us rays of hope. Let death, however, find us alive!

If you give us your hand, we will have nothing to fear. Rather, in the last instant of our life, we will experience death as our entrance into the cathedral glowing with light, the end of a long pilgrimage with a burning lamp. Entering the sanctuary after putting the lamp out, we will set it down because we will no longer need the light of faith to illumine our path. The glory of the Lord will be our light (cf. Rev 21:23). We pray you, help us so that we might live our death this way.

Holy Mary, the Gospel tells us that Jesus bowed his head when he gave up his spirit on the cross. As many artists have portrayed, he probably bowed his head onto yours, in the same attitude of abandon he had as a baby when sleep overtook him.

Upright under the cross, perhaps standing on a stone pedestal, you became his cushion at death.

When our time comes to give ourselves over to the Father, and none of those present can respond to our pleas, as we sink into that loneliness which even our dearest loved ones cannot fill, offer us your head as our last cushion.

In that last instant of life, the warmth of your face will evoke from the never-opened tombs of our unconsciousness another instant—the first after birth when we experienced the warmth of another maternal face. Perhaps only then, even with the faint light of a mind going dark, we will understand that the pains of our agony are merely the pangs of a new birth.

Holy Mary, prepare us for that great voyage. Help us to resolve, with true repentance and a plea of forgiveness, the final matters regarding God's justice. Ask for us the benefits of amnesty, which God bestows with royal mercy. Help us to put all in order so that when we reach the gates of paradise, they will open for us when we knock.

Then, we will finally enter the kingdom, accompanied by the echo of the *Stabat Mater*. With our sad yet hopeful accents, we have asked for your protection and have sung its refrain so many times at the end of the Way of the Cross: "When our body dies, let the glory of paradise be given to our soul. Amen."

Chapter 31
COMPANION ON OUR JOURNEY

Holy Mary, tender and strong mother, you accompany us on our journey along the roads of life. Whenever we contemplate the great things God has done in you, we feel such remorse over our sluggishness. We want to try to lengthen our steps so we can walk alongside you.

Accept our wish to take your hand, and increase the pace of such weary travelers. As pilgrims in faith, we seek the Lord's face and contemplate you as an icon of human solicitude toward those in need. In haste, we will reach the "city," and bring the needy the same fruits of joy that you brought to Elizabeth.

Holy Mary, virgin of the morning, give us the joy of sensing, even under the mist of dawn, the hopes of the new day. Inspire in us words of courage. Don't let our voice tremble when, despite the great malice and sins which age the world, we dare to proclaim that better times will come. On our lips, do not allow complaints to prevail over wonder; do not let skepticism crush enthusiasm. May the weight of the past never hinder us from drawing credit on the future. Help us to rely on young people with more daring, and preserve us from the temptation to flatter them with sterile words. Only our authenticity and consistency will attract them. Multiply our energies so that we might know how to invest them in the only business still profitable on the market of civilization: the protection of new generations from the atrocious evils which now shorten earth's breath. Give to our voices the joy of the Easter alleluia. Fill with dreams the sands of our realism. Help us to understand that it counts more to point out the buds sprouting on branches than to lament the fallen leaves. Fill us with the security of those who already see the east gloriously ablaze with the first rays of the sun.

Holy Mary, virgin of midday, give us the gladness of the light. We find too often that our lights have gone out. Remove us from the desolation of confusion and inspire in us the humility of inquiry. Water our drought of grace in the palm of your hand. Bring us to the faith which another mother—poor and good like you—passed on to us when we were children, and which we may have carelessly sold for a wretched plate of lentils. You, beggar of the spirit, fill our jars with oil destined to burn before God; we have already let them burn too long before our idols in the desert. Help us to abandon ourselves to him.

Temper our spirit of pride. Let not the light of faith—even when it takes on accents of prophetic denunciation—make us arrogant or presumptuous. Rather, let it give us the joy of tolerance and understanding. But above all, free us from the tragedy that our belief in God might remain alien to the concrete choices of each moment, whether public or private, and run the risk of never becoming flesh and blood on the altar of our working days.

Holy Mary, virgin of the evening, Mother of the hour when we return home and taste the joy of being accepted, sharing the gladness of sitting at supper with others, give us the gift of communion. We ask it for our Church in order that it may grow in the unity the Lord prayed for. We ask it for our city, often reduced to a battleground by factions. We ask it for our families, so that dialogue and self-sacrificing love will make them privileged places of Christian and civil growth. We ask it for ourselves so that, far from selfishness and isolation, we might always stand on the side of life. We ask it for the entire world, so that solidarity among peoples may be rediscovered as the only ethical imperative on which to base human society. Let the poor take their places, with equal dignity, at the table of all, and let peace be the aim of our daily tasks.

Holy Mary, virgin of the night, we implore you to stay close when grief strikes us and when trials beset us. Free us from the terror of shadows. At the hour of our Calvary, may you, who experienced the eclipse of the sun, spread your cloak over us. Wrapped in your breath, the long wait for freedom will be more bearable. Lighten with a mother's touch the sufferings of the sick. Fill with your tender and discreet presence the bitter times of the lonely. Help weary travelers, and offer them your shoulder so they might rest their head. Keep from all harm our loved ones working in distant places, and comfort with the strengthening glance of your eyes, anyone who has lost trust in life. Repeat today your *Magnificat,* and announce an abundance of justice to all those oppressed on earth. Do not leave us alone in the night to sing of our fears. Rather, if you come close to us in the darkness and whisper that you too are waiting for the light, the tears will dry on our faces. Then we will wake the dawn together. Amen.

Pauline
BOOKS & MEDIA

The Daughters of St. Paul operate book and media centers at the following addresses. Visit, call or write the one nearest you today, or find us on the World Wide Web, www.pauline.org

CALIFORNIA
3908 Sepulveda Blvd, Culver City, CA
   90230   310-397-8676
5945 Balboa Avenue, San Diego, CA
   92111   858-565-9181
46 Geary Street, San Francisco, CA
   94108   415-781-5180

FLORIDA
145 S.W. 107th Avenue, Miami, FL
   33174   305-559-6715

HAWAII
1143 Bishop Street, Honolulu, HI
   96813   808-521-2731
Neighbor Islands call:
   800-259-8463

ILLINOIS
172 North Michigan Avenue, Chicago,
   IL 60601   312-346-4228

LOUISIANA
4403 Veterans Memorial Blvd,
   Metairie, LA 70006   504-887-7631

MASSACHUSETTS
Rte. 1, 885 Providence Hwy, Dedham,
   MA 02026   781-326-5385

MISSOURI
9804 Watson Road, St. Louis, MO
   63126   314-965-3512

NEW JERSEY
561 U.S. Route 1, Wick Plaza,
   Edison, NJ 08817   732-572-1200

NEW YORK
150 East 52nd Street, New York, NY
   10022   212-754-1110
78 Fort Place, Staten Island, NY
   10301   718-447-5071

OHIO
2105 Ontario Street, Cleveland, OH
   44115   216-621-9427

PENNSYLVANIA
9171-A Roosevelt Blvd, Philadelphia,
   PA 19114   215-676-9494

SOUTH CAROLINA
243 King Street, Charleston, SC
   29401   843-577-0175

TENNESSEE
4811 Poplar Avenue, Memphis, TN
   38117   901-761-2987

TEXAS
114 Main Plaza, San Antonio, TX
   78205   210-224-8101

VIRGINIA
1025 King Street, Alexandria, VA
   22314   703-549-3806

CANADA
3022 Dufferin Street, Toronto,
   Ontario, Canada M6B 3T5
   416-781-9131
1155 Yonge Street, Toronto,
   Ontario, Canada M4T 1W2
   416-934-3440

¡También somos su fuente para libros, videos y música en español!